# proclamation 2

**Aids for Interpreting the
Lessons of the Church Year**

**Ernest W. Saunders
and
Fred B. Craddock**

series b

editors: Elizabeth Achtemeier · Gerhard Krodel · Charles P. Price

**FORTRESS PRESS**          **PHILADELPHIA**

COPYRIGHT © 1981 BY FORTRESS PRESS

---

**Library of Congress Cataloging in Publication Data** (Revised)
Main entry under title:

Proclamation 2.

Consists of 24 Volumes in 3 series designated A, B, and C which correspond to the cycles of the three year lectionary plus 4 volumes covering the lesser festivals. Each series contains 8 basic volumes with the following titles: Advent-Christmas, Epiphany, Lent, Holy Week, Easter, Pentecost 1, Pentecost 2, and Pentecost 3.
    CONTENTS: [etc.]—Series C: [1] Fuller, R. H. Advent-Christmas. [2] Pervo, R. I. and Carl III, W. J. Epiphany.—Thulin, R. L. et. al. The lesser festivals. 4 v.
    1. Bible—Homiletical use. 2. Bible—Liturgical lessons, English.
[BS534.5.P76]    251    79–7377
ISBN 0–8006–4079–9 (ser. C, v. 1)

---

# Contents

# Editor's Foreword

This volume of Proclamation 2 supplies exegetical and homiletical interpretations of the lessons appointed for the Epiphany season during Cycle B of the common lectionary.

As much as Good Friday has to do with the atonement, Easter with the resurrection, or Pentecost with the Spirit, Epiphany focuses on revelation. The word revelation means manifestation or coming to light. The feast itself is celebrated on January 6 (the date of the winter solstice, according to an Egyptian calendar so old at the beginning of the Christian era that it was already sixteen days out of phase with the astronomical events of which it was designed to keep track). At the solstice, the sun reaches its nadir and turns north again. Days grow longer. Light is born. Thus the solstice has always seemed a natural symbol for the birth of Christ, the Light of the World. Eastern churches adopted the January date for the birth of Jesus long before Western churches settled for December 25—another solstice date—in the fourth century. In the West, January 6 has been retained as the commemoration of the coming of the Magi, "following yonder star," to worship the Christ child in Bethlehem. Among us, January 6 is the "Manifestation of Christ to the Gentiles." We too have come to the light.

The baptism of Jesus, with its story of the voice from heaven declaring the identity of Jesus as the divine Son, and the descent of the Spirit upon him, is another manifestation story. It has long been celebrated in connection with the Epiphany as the beginning of Jesus' public ministry. In the calendar on which our lessons are based, the Baptism of Our Lord is always celebrated on the First Sunday after Epiphany.

The season varies in length, depending on the date of Easter. If Easter is late, Epiphany may have as many as nine Sundays; if Easter is early, it may have as few as four. Whether long or short, Epiphany is a time of revelation. The successive Sundays bring into focus successive manifestations of Jesus as the Christ as these are recorded in the Gospels: his teaching, his preaching to the poor, and his ministry of healing. All these deeds are epiphanies of the Lord. In cycle B we live through them as they are contained in the Second Gospel, the Gospel according to Mark.

The last Sunday after Epiphany, the Sunday before Ash Wednesday, is always devoted to the Transfiguration of the Lord, his manifestation to Peter, James, and John as God's divine Son, just before he turned his face to Jerusalem and the cross. It is an appropriate introduction to Lent.

The exegetical portion of this volume has been prepared with both precision and affection by Ernest W. Saunders, Dean and Professor of New Testament Interpretation (Emeritus) at Garrett Theological Seminary. He is the author of *Jesus in the Gospels* and *John Celebrates the Gospel* and has edited a number of New Testament manuscripts from Mount Athos. The homiletical interpretation by Fred P. Craddock turns the exegesis toward the particular task of the preacher, with a skillful eye both to the meaning of the text as Professor Saunders sets it before us and to the meaning of the Epiphany of Our Lord in this year of grace in the United States. Dr. Craddock is Professor of Religion at Emory University and the author of *Overhearing the Gospel* (the Lyman Beecher lectures for 1978), and *The Pre-Existence of Christ*.

CHARLES P. PRICE

# Editor's Note

The extrabiblical literature referred to in this volume covers a wide range of ancient primary sources not readily available to the generalist: Classical Greek and Latin authors, Hellenistic Greek and Jewish texts, postbiblical Jewish literature, and early Christian documents. Much of this literature has increasingly been studied by biblical scholars in order to see the Bible in the broad context of antiquity.

# The Epiphany of Our Lord

| Lutheran | Roman Catholic | Episcopal | Pres/UCC/Chr | Meth/COCU |
|----------|----------------|-----------|--------------|-----------|
| Isa. 60:1–6 | Isa. 60:1–6 | Isa. 60:1–6, 9 | Isa. 60:1–6 | Isa. 60:1–6 |
| Eph. 3:2–21 | Eph. 3:2–3, 5–6 | Eph. 3:1–12 | Eph. 3:1–6 | Eph. 3:1–12 |
| Matt. 2:1–12 | Matt. 2:1–12 | Matt. 2:1–12 | Matt. 2:1–12 | Matt. 2:1–12 |

## EXEGESIS

*First Lesson: Isa. 60:1–6.* The OT passage to be read on Epiphany Sunday is commonly recognized to be a segment of the message of the so-called Second Isaiah, or, alternatively, an even later voice sometimes called Third Isaiah (Isaiah 56—66). In these chapters, it is possible to detect not only the basic themes, and on occasion even the exact language of Second Isaiah (Isaiah 40—55), but also some significant differences. The return of some of the Jewish exiles from Babylon is now an historical fact. Jerusalem is in some measure restored. The prospect of these events had been joyously anticipated by Second Isaiah. Now, amidst economic hardships and the staggering tasks of reconstruction, it is evident that the restoration of Zion was not the occasion of Yahweh's blessing and honor.

The certainty of salvation in the face of this present desolation is the unqualified conviction and message of this prophet. Apart from one somber word (60:12), he sings of a deliverance, wrought by a miraculous act of God on behalf of his suffering people, that will be of universal scope and will usher in a new day for all humanity.

Echoing the language of Isa. 9:2, he speaks of the advent of Yahweh as light breaking in upon the darkness that has covered the land. Darkness is the sign of death, as light is the sign of life (Ps. 13:3) and of the presence of Yahweh (Ps. 27:1). Where God is, there is salvation/life for his people (Isa. 56:1; 59:11; 60:1; 62:11; 63:4; 66:15; and again Ps. 27:1). Who then can be dismayed or fearful or believe he is abandoned?

God's coming is seen as a light rising like a star upon his people (v. 1), a light that will be reflected so others may see and come to share the glory (v. 2). Borrowing the language of his teacher, the author tells the community that more of their sons and daughters will come back home and that their captors and other foreigners will come with them (v. 4; cf. 49:18). These people and their kings will gratefully and joyfully bring their own treasures to offer to the God of Israel, who will be recognized as the God of all nations.

The new word in this manifestation of God to humanity (epiphany) is that he comes not as an agent of judgment or vengeance, but as the bringer of salvation. He comes to his covenanted people, Israel, and the nations of the earth join them to come before his presence. They come out of the captivity of darkness into the freedom of light; from a condition of sovereign states in contest each with the other to an inclusive community under God. Human fantasy or divine destiny? This prophet of the early Persian period surely stands with those in Judaism and Christianity who affirm the latter belief. Twenty-five centuries later, in this season of Epiphany, it is still a breathtaking prospect.

*Second Lesson: Eph. 3:1–12.* In the form of an autobiographical parenthesis, the Second Lesson presents Paul's understanding of his ministry, the heart of the gospel, and the mission of the church. The writer, whether the apostle himself or, as it seems more likely, a faithful disciple, believes that the good news of God's program of redemption was disclosed in Jesus Christ. A full account of that holy intention has heretofore been hidden from human understanding, but now it has been made manifest. It is a mystery cleared up; a secret no longer hidden but declared to the holy apostles, to Spirit-inspired prophets, and, assuredly, to the master missionary himself. Nowhere is it more succinctly put than in the thematic statement of purpose: "to unite all things in him (Christ), things in heaven and things on earth" (1:10); that is to say, his resolute purpose is to bring creation to new creation, a fulfillment that can best be defined in the new reality of Christ who is the center and the summing up (*anakephalaiōsasthai*) of the whole universe (*ta panta*).

In our lesson, this summary statement is elaborated. V. 6 sets it out: Divine redemption is offered as an equal opportunity to everyone, irrespective of ethnic origin or religious affiliation. "Gentiles are fellow heirs [not second-class citizens], members of the same body [not separate but equal], and partakers [on an equal basis] of the promise in Christ Jesus"—this is the gospel. There is not one word for the Jews and another for the Gentiles. It is one word of salvation spoken to everyone who will hear.

These words describe what has been actually happening in the ministry of the risen Christ during Paul's lifetime, through his church. The divine determination to rescue persons from death and bring them to life has become "*realized* in Christ Jesus our Lord" (v. 11).

V. 10 should be seen as critically important for an understanding of the mission of the church in the world. The strange references to "principalities and powers in the heavenly places" is a way of speaking about *the world* in its disobedience to and alienation from God (cf. 2:2; 6:12). The church is seen as the instrument of God active in the world—combating alien forces, making known the truth about creation and redemption, declaring the "manifold wisdom of God" to this hostile world and its powers. How is that done? Through the boldness of speech mentioned in v. 12 and the references to active resistance in 6:12ff. These verses suggest that Christian presence must be interpreted as prophetic preaching and action undertaken to overcome unbelief and disobedience and to unite *all* things, including even the hostile powers (Col. 1:18–20), in Christ. That's a NT mandate for prophetic mission!

*Gospel: Matt: 2:1–12.* The story of the expected savior-king of Israel should be read in the context of the hope of a divine deliverer that was widespread in the Mediterranean world of the Hellenistic and Roman empires. This hope is found in the Persian oracle of Hystaspes and the Brahman Yasht, in the Egyptian Demotic Chronicle and the Potter's Oracle, and in the Roman poet Virgil's *Fourth Eclogue.*

Jewish literature of the period also evokes dreams of a gladsome day of deliverance and the establishment of God's rule through his vicegerent. In particular Third Isaiah, as we have already seen, heralds that great day when not only will Zion be triumphant but the nations of the world with their rulers will make pilgrimage to Jerusalem (for example, Isa. 60:3, 6; cf. 49:12; Ps. 72:10f.). The Torah oracle of Balaam about a victorious king who is called "a star out of Jacob" (Num. 24:17) became a messianic prophecy applied to such personages as the Righteous Teacher of Qumran (CD 7.18ff.; 1QM 11.6) and to Simeon bar Kozibah, the leader of the Second Jewish Revolt (A.D. 132-135).

It is significant that Matthew does not refer to these Jewish expectations; instead he makes *Gentiles* the seekers after the world deliverer and the recipients of the revelation. A group of priest-astrologers (*Magi*) coming from some Eastern country visits King Herod in Jerusalem, in search of the Jewish ruler destined to become the divine deliverer. Consulting men learned in the Law and the tradition of his people, Herod advises them that Bethlehem, David's birthplace, will be the birthplace of David's successor, the Messiah of Israel (Mic. 5:2). The priests make their way joyfully to the Judean town while the king begins his scheming for the elimination of this possible rival.

What the prophetic oracles describe as an event of the future—the coming of the ideal king as savior of a stricken humanity—Matthew and the church declare to be an historical reality. Emmanuel has come! The evangelist is saying, in effect, that the Jews rejected the revelation but that the Gentiles have accepted it. The Gospel story understands that God does not leave himself without witness among the nations (Acts 14:17): The Magi recognize the portents of his coming. But more, these heathen prophecies are ambiguous and uncertain. Matthew implies that they can only be clarified and comprehended in the light of Hebrew prophecy and the gospel. The story has a kerygmatic rather than historical function. The coming of Jesus is an eschatological event. It is the fulfillment of the hopes and dreams of God's people among all the nations of the earth. It is happening in the phenomenon of the church in the evangelist's day.

## HOMILETICAL INTERPRETATION

The governing thought and mood of this season of the church year is "epiphany": the manifestation, appearance, and revelation of Jesus Christ. This revelation is the magnet which the preacher will hold over the texts for today and the nine Sundays that follow. All the texts are so rich that minor themes will tempt the preacher down delightful detours and side trails, and those who take these trips can certainly find adequate resources for a clear and certain word. But let us keep Epiphany throughout the season, announcing the appearance of our Lord. We need very much to hear it and to say it: Emmanuel, "God is with us."

This is not to imply that all three texts for a given Sunday will move with equal ease to the magnet, nor should one feel somehow compelled to force them to do so. However, the preacher will want to guard against being seduced by those texts which seem to offer their meanings with such facility and immediacy that the others, by neglect, are left in obscurity. The interpreter of Scripture knows that some of the richest veins await the one willing to dig deeper. After all, the Epiphany of Jesus Christ was not obvious. His appearance among us was and is concealed as well as revealed. His coming was and is a mystery discerned, a secret shared, a whispered shout, an event lying between the vulgarity of the totally transparent and the cruelty of the totally opaque. As the Fourth Gospel expresses it, Jesus heard God's voice answer his prayer, but some standing by said it thundered (John 12:27–29). The preacher respects this quality in the text and continues it in the texture of the sermon.

In the lection for this Sunday, clear kinship between Isaiah 60 and Matthew 2 is evident. Matthew has nourished his narrative with the beautiful images of the prophet: as a bright star on a dark night, God appears to restore and redeem his people; the nations shall be drawn to this light and will share in God's salvation; with gold and frankincense, nations shall come to worship and praise God. These two texts weave so rich a tapestry that one is tempted to use Ephesians 3 only as a reading for the day, without comments. But upon more careful investigation, all three texts join in several clear announcements.

First, God's saving work in the world often comes through times, places, and means that surprise even the faithful. Isaiah's song of God's reclaiming

10 Epiphany—Series B

his creation comes out of a most unlikely context. The magnificent promise
of the return of the exiles to the ancient homeland had been lost in the
poverty of its fullfillment. Relatively few returned to build the new
Jerusalem, and their work lay heavy in their hands. Discouraged, over-
worked, surrounded by enemies, and deprived economically, these hud-
dled pilgrims now feel they have every reason for doubt and anger. But it is
the prophet's surprising announcement that here and now, through these
very people, God is beginning the reconciliation of the world to himself.
Likewise, those addressed by the Ephesian Letter had every reason to
believe that their primary goal was to survive as a church. How few they
were in that huge pagan world! New members were hard to come by,
considering that their message centered upon a cross and service. And
realistically speaking, who would dream that their acts of kindness and
words of love without regard to race or sex or class could possibly make
even a crack in the dark and ancient walls between Jews and Gentiles, slave
and free, male and female? "That's the way life is," some could sigh.
"Maybe God never intended for us to be together," others could ponder.
And yet, says the writer, it is precisely through this church that God will
implement his purpose: the uniting of all persons in Christ Jesus. And in the
day's Gospel, the inhabitants of Bethlehem had every reason to greet the
new day as they had greeted the day before and the day before that, beyond
all memory: May the heel of the enemy not crush us today. The Roman
soldier rattles his sword, the Jewish traitor collects the taxes, the puppet
government compromises the faith of Abraham. Surely God has forgotten
us. But it was to this little town that the Magi came with gifts for the King
before whom someday every knee would bow. In short, all three texts
remind us that God is God, that God has the power and the willingness to
accomplish his purpose. A gospel that does not begin and end in this
confidence is no gospel at all but rather a warm wish that things were
different, a small dish of melted grace that will hardly nourish anyone who
watches the evening news.

Second, God's epiphany is for the healing and restoring of all people. We
have already seen and heard this in the prophet's vision, in the coming of
the Magi, and in the unveiling of the mystery of God's purpose to create one
human community in Jesus Christ. But the preacher will probably find
expressions such as "all nations" or "human community" too nameless
and too faceless to effect more than a drowsy consent. The sermon should
zoom in like a camera for a closeup of the membership of God's church.
Only then can the listeners experience the surprise and shock at the power
of the gospel to overcome racial, social, cultural, and economic barriers.
Open the doors to Matthew's church: His pews are filled with "the good
and the bad." Luke's roll lists "poor, lame, halt, and blind." Paul's

preaching gathered "Jew and Greek, bond and free, wise and foolish, male and female." Or read only the Acts of the Apostles: You attend the baptisms of Jews, Samaritans, Roman soldiers, a businesswoman from Asia, an orator from Egypt, a eunuch in the service of an Ethopian queen, noblewomen of Greece, household servants, as well as a host of peddlers, fortunetellers, tent makers, city officials, and nameless indigents from Rome to Damascus. This was a membership roll defined by the gospel, not by the politics, prejudices, economics, or education of the general culture. Can that church still be found?

Third, there is powerful opposition to this redemptive purpose of God. From the time of Isaiah to the present, some in the believing community have made it clear that those who are "different from us" are not welcome. These people are proud of our church and plan to keep it *ours*. And outside the church, Herod is still very much alive, screaming death threats, sending the sword to clear the streets, while vultures circle over the shallow graves of the innocent. He admits to no open persecution of Christians, of course, but simply "the price that has to be paid for law and order." Never before in the history of the church has there been such widespread persecution of Christians: intimidation; threat to property, job, and life; imprisonment without fair trial; execution. It may be that churches in America have become so enamored of small groups and intimate circles for therapeutic sharing that the larger mission involving inevitable clashes with the structures of evil has been dropped through inattention from the job description of what it is to be the church. The author of the Ephesian Letter understands this opposition to God's reclaiming the world in love as a force far deeper and stronger than disinterested society, immoral life styles, or unsympathetic governments. In the culture of that letter, the power of evil in the world was so dark, mysterious, and overwhelming as to be attributed to principalities and powers, demons that pervade the universe and seek to thwart the will of God. Most of us do not believe in demons, but our enlightened view has not reduced noticeably the forces that corrupt and cripple human bodies, minds, and spirits. It is an inescapable fact that Christian living and Christian ministry include the posture of "over against." Jesus announced his ministry as one of preaching good news to the poor, releasing captives, liberating the oppressed, and opening the eyes of the blind. Who could possibly oppose such healing and relieving work? Apparently someone had other plans for the poor, imprisoned, blind, and oppressed, because there were the constant hassles. And the cross.

If anyone imagined that Epiphany is the proclamation that wherever the Christ appears there is no pain or grief, then our texts correct the illusion. The truth lies in the reverse: Wherever there is pain and grief, there is the Christ, Emmanuel.

# The Baptism of Our Lord
# The First Sunday after the Epiphany

| Lutheran | Roman Catholic | Episcopal | Pres/UCC/Chr | Meth/COCU |
|---|---|---|---|---|
| Isa. 42:1–7 | Isa. 42:1–4, 6–7 | Isa. 42:1–9 | Isa. 61:1–4 | Isa. 42:1–9 |
| Acts 10:34–38 | Acts 10:34–38 | Acts 10:34–38 | Acts 11:4–18 | Acts 10:34–38 |
| Mark 1:4–11 | Mark 1:7–11 | Mark 1:7–11 | Mark 1:4–11 | Mark 1:4–11 |

## EXEGESIS

*First Lesson: Isa. 61:1–4.* The autobiographical statements in Isaiah 61 offer a unique account of an unknown postexilic prophet's call to mission and his understanding of the tasks that are involved. It has been said that this is "the last occasion in the history of Israel on which a prophet expressed his certainty of having been sent by God with a message to his nation with such freedom and conviction" (C. Westermann, *Isaiah Forty— Sixty Six: A Commentary* [Philadelphia: Westminster Press, 1969], p. 367).

The call is interpreted as a miraculous endowment with the Spirit of God (cf. Isa. 42:1b; Mic. 3:8), associated with an anointing. Elsewhere, however, the act of anointing is associated only with kings, and Spirit-empowerment, if assumed, is not specified. This prophet's task is to bring a message, an action word which becomes an event, bringing about a change. Good tidings (the Greek equivalent is *evangelion*, gospel) are brought to the afflicted. The brokenhearted are to be healed. Captives are to be released. The prophet is divinely appointed to proclaim the era of divine mercy and forgiveness upon this disconsolate and defeated people.

Whereas the national situation prior to the catastrophe of Jerusalem's fall called for sharp warnings of an approaching doom by the preexilic prophets, the human circumstance now required consolation and encouragement to a people for whom hopelessness was the daily reality. This prophet sees a new day beyond the present predicament of Israel, but nonetheless close at hand—close enough to shore up their sagging spirits and inspire fresh courage. In the grand design of Yahweh, those who now mourn will rejoice (v. 3), their faintheartedness replaced by acts of praise, so that once again they will be a sturdy people, secure in God.

Because of Yahweh's attitude of grace and blessing, it will become possible to rebuild the ruined cities of the land (v. 4). This in fact was already beginning to happen. This prophet interprets the physical facts of restoration, begun and yet to be completed, as evidence that judgment is done and Zion again is enjoying God's favor. Centuries later the church was to understand his call to ministry as fulfilled in the work of Jesus of Nazareth (Luke 4:16–30).

*Second Lesson: Acts 11:4–18.* The scene is set in a conclave of the Jewish Christian church of Jerusalem, including the apostles, assembled to hear Peter's views on why he maintains free relationships and table fellowships with Gentiles in Caesarea. Though the accusation centers on the violation of Jewish dietary restrictions, it is obvious that Luke, the author, sees the issue at stake here as the eligibility of all persons, Jews and Gentiles, to be baptized and to receive "repentance unto life," or salvation (10:28; 11:18).

The account in this pericope of the baptism of Cornelius by Peter cannot be comprehended in itself; it presupposes the reader's familiarity with the full story in 10:1–48, of which this defense by Peter before the church leaders is an epitome. Testifying with him are six brothers from the church of Joppa who themselves were eyewitnesses to the extraordinary event of this Roman officer's conversion and baptism (v. 12; cf. 10:23). It is clear that this "Gentile Pentecost," as it has been termed, is considered by Luke to be a pivotal event in the story of the penetration of the gospel into the world. The threefold repetition of the vision (notice 10:16 and 11:10) and the emphasis on the piety of the officer (10:2, 4, 22, 31) display Luke's technique for stressing the importance of this event. Luke is deeply convinced that the church's mission to the Gentiles is not of human devising but grounded in God and divinely directed and maintained. For Luke, Peter is a central figure in this God-inspired mission, as he was also in the matter of coming to faith in the risen Lord (Luke 22:31–32). For Luke what matters is not the chronology but the theology of mission.

*Gospel: Mark 1:4–11.* The evangelist, and with him the whole early church, understands John the baptizer as the beginning of the new salvation time, the forerunner of the Messiah, Jesus, fulfilling the eschatological role often associated in Jewish expectation with Elijah. Like Jesus and Jesus' disciples, John too preached. Mark and Luke do not shrink from assuming that John preached "the gospel" (Mark 1:1; Luke 3:18).

That John the Baptist was a controversial figure is borne out by the variety of estimates preserved in the tradition. To Christians, he was clearly the precursor of Jesus in God's redemptive purpose. His contemporaries saw him as a prophetic figure (Mark 11:32), or the Prophet expected in the last times (Mark 9:13; Matt. 11:14; Luke 7:26); or the Prophet-Messiah (Luke 1:76). Among his followers he may have been recognized as the Messiah (Luke 3:15f.; John 1:19–27; Acts 13:25; Pseudo-Clementine Recognitions I, 60).

John comes on the scene in the Judean desert, preaching a message of radical change (repentance, *metanoia*), righteousness (*dikaiosynē*, Matt. 21:32), and renewal (forgiveness, *aphēsis*). The desert had been the escape corridor for the Exodus from Egypt into the Promised Land. On the promise of Isa. 40:3, a new exodus was anticipated in the last times. John's nomadic attire and daily diet accent his message and ceremonial act of baptism in enlisting penitents who are prepared for these final events.

The turning away from sin (the larger meaning of *metanoia*), the repudiation of a life style that took little or no account of God, and the acceptance of God's righteous judgment, signified in the baptismal act, offered to the truly penitent the assurance of divine forgiveness. For John this is the eschatological forgiveness, promised by the prophets, which marks God's action at the close of the age (Isa. 33:24; 40:2; 53:5, 6; Jer. 31:34; Ezek. 36:25). This is preliminary to and anticipatory of the baptism by the Messiah, the "Mightier One," who was yet to appear: "He will baptize you with the Holy Spirit" (v. 8). The older form of this baptismal saying is undoubtedly preserved by Matthew and Luke who describe it as "Holy Spirit and fire" (Matt. 3:11; Luke 3:16). By baptism with wind (Spirit) and fire, the Baptizer probably understood the final act of God's judgment executed through his Anointed One.

But the church knew this judgment as already active (Rom. 1:18), and that baptism meant not simply judgment, but the supreme gift of the Holy Spirit to cleanse and empower human life. This is the way the church came to understand John's eschatological preaching.

### HOMILETICAL INTERPRETATION

If the preacher keeps in mind the central meaning of Epiphany, then the sermon for this Sunday may well center on Jesus' baptism in the Gospel accounts. The baptism of Jesus by John in the Jordan River was understood by the early church as an occasion of divine revelation with threefold attestation: the splitting of the heavens (a sign of the breaking-in of a new age), the coming of the power of the Holy Spirit upon Jesus, and the voice of God's approval as Jesus launches his ministry by identifying with John's call to prepare for the approaching kingdom. The account in Mark 1:4–11 attracted to itself Isa. 61:1–4 and Acts 11:4–18. That which unites these texts is the outpouring of the Holy Spirit. To focus upon baptism and the Holy Spirit in one sermon will not call for any special homiletical gymnastics; the two are repeatedly joined in the NT. The happy union of these texts should enable the preacher to lift both the act of baptism and the gift of the Holy Spirit out of the subjective captivity that has tended in many quarters to shrink the grand themes of our faith into private feelings and warm fuzzies.

Jesus' baptism did, indeed, have a personal and private dimension. The voice from heaven, says Mark, was addressed to Jesus, not to the crowd: "*You* are my beloved Son." But its meaning for Jesus or for us is hardly exhausted by musing on how Jesus felt at the time. Mark sets this baptism into the larger context of God's purpose in the world. Having set the scene of John's ministry as that of a new exodus (Isa. 40:3), Mark climaxes the narrative with the coming of Jesus to the Jordan for baptism. That event itself is interpreted as the beginning of the new age and the newly baptized Jesus is approved by the heavenly voice with descriptive phrases from a coronation of the king (Psalm 2) and the commissioning of the suffering servant (Isaiah 42). Thus sovereignty and service are joined in this act which fulfills the old and launches the new. Evidently the church preserved this account not solely because it said something important about Jesus, but also because it said something important about baptism as the church practiced and interpreted it. On this assumption, baptism is not only a rite of initiation, not only a signal moment in one's relation to God as a child of God, but it is also a time of becoming a character in the ongoing story of God's work in the world. In addition, it is an act of participation in the eschatological age, the time of the consummation of God's purpose for his people. And between that history and that hope, baptism is a commissioning, an ordination to ministry. To be ordained to ministry is to affirm one's baptismal vows, and to that the whole church has been called and set apart.

The Gospel account of Jesus' baptism is joined by the two other lections for today in focusing on the coming of the Holy Spirit. The preacher will doubtless want to reflect upon the wide difference between the descriptions of the function of the Holy Spirit in these texts and those texts which have become very popular in much of the current discussion about the Holy Spirit. For reasons not altogether clear, there has been in recent years a surge of interest in the gifts, the *charismata,* of the Spirit. Of Paul's two primary lists of these gifts, Romans 12 and 1 Corinthians 12, the more unusual and mysterious (1 Corinthians 12) has received by far the greater amount of attention. And even though Paul insists in both passages that these gifts are for ministry and service, very often interest has not been prompted or sustained by a search for ways and means of service. These and other texts have been seized by those who need assurances of God's love, proofs of salvation, evidences of a new birth or second blessing, grounds for witnessing that "I really am saved," or similar personal experiences of God's love. This hunger is most often genuine, and the extent to which it has not been addressed or satisfied may be an indictment of the churches. But to think or cause others to think that this is the only or even the primary description of the role of the Holy Spirit offered by the Scripture is a gross and grievous error.

Look again at the texts for today. The prophet was called to minister to the returnees from the Exile. Few in number, economically deprived, socially ostracized, and growing increasingly disheartened, these people needed ministry desperately. They needed a word which assured them that the call to return was really God's call, that what they had begun would bear fruit, that their work was not in vain but had meaning beyond the dismal moment. In order that he might carry out this ministry, the prophet received the Spirit of God; he was anointed and endowed to bring good news of release, healing, and hope. The Spirit came to equip and to commission for God's service. Centuries later, Jesus would claim this text as the characterization of his own ministry (Luke 4:16–21). Likewise, in Mark's account of Jesus' baptism the Holy Spirit came upon Jesus, anointing and empowering him for ministry. Following a period of intense struggle, Jesus went into Galilee preaching, teaching, and casting out demons.

Within the context of ministry but with a different accent, the work of the Holy Spirit is described in Acts 11:4–18. Simon Peter had interrupted a preaching tour in Joppa in order to follow a vision—and a series of most unusual coincidences—to Caesarea where he, contrary to his own preferences and prejudices and contrary to the practice of his church, ate with, preached to, and baptized some Gentiles. For this Peter was criticized in the Jerusalem Church. Peter recited the events, confessing to his own reticence all the way. However, he said, when it was evident that God had poured out upon those Gentiles the same Spirit which had been given us, "who was I that I could withstand God?" Here again the Holy Spirit is associated with ministry and mission but also pushes us beyond the barriers of our racial and social prejudices to see and experience the breadth of God's embrace. Herein lies the possibility of a charismatic movement that has never yet really gripped the church.

# The Second Sunday after the Epiphany

| Lutheran | Roman Catholic | Episcopal | Pres/UCC/Chr | Meth/COCU |
|---|---|---|---|---|
| 1 Sam. 3:1–10 | 1 Sam. 3:3b–10, 19 | 1 Sam. 3:1–10, (11–20) | 1 Sam. 3:1–10 | 1 Sam. 3:1–20 |
| 1 Cor. 6:12–20 | 1 Cor. 6:13c–15a, 17–20 | 1 Cor. 6:11b–20 | 1 Cor. 6:12–20 | 1 Cor. 6:11b–20 |
| John 1:43–51 | John 1:35–42 | John 1:43–51 | John 1:35–42 | John 1:35–51 |

## EXEGESIS

*First Lesson: 1 Sam. 3:1–20.* The call of the prophet Samuel is an episode in the Samuel-Saul-David story. Samuel, of course, figures in the earlier accounts of the establishment of the monarchy, but in the later tradition he plays a more prominent part as the true man of God who chose and ordained Saul as the first king of Israel, and who chose David as his successor. Samuel was dedicated as an infant to the service of Yahweh and grew up under the tutelage of the priest, Eli, officiant at the sanctuary at Shiloh in southern Samaria. The parallelism between the stories of the boy Samuel ministering in the temple and the boy Jesus teaching in the temple cannot escape notice. It is likely that Luke is using a story that has been shaped in part by this ancient account of an unusual child marked for a special religious destiny. Later Jewish tradition speaks of the age of Samuel at the time of his call as having been twelve years of age, as does the Christian tradition speak of Jesus, probably relating the experiences with the passage from childhood to manhood *(bar mitzwāh)*.

Samuel, at the dawn of young manhood, is called to declare the word of the Lord against the house of Eli. It is a fourfold summons, unidentified at first but recognized by the aged priest Eli as a divine summons. The rousing of Samuel from sleep three times to go to the priest accentuates the mysterious and supernatural character of the experience. As it was for other prophets, the message to Samuel was one of stern judgment, a sentence of doom upon the custodian of the sanctuary and upon his whole family. Their arrogant and unlawful administration at this famous Ephraim- ite shrine at Shiloh was offensive to Yahweh. Samuel thus takes his place with the long line of prophets *(nebi'im)* who stand out against the injustice and infidelity of their people as rugged advocates of the one and true God of Israel.

*Second Lesson: 1 Cor. 6:12–20.* In chapters 5 and 6 of this letter to the Christian community at Corinth the apostle is grappling with several as- pects of the Christian's relationship to the wider culture, what Paul terms the world. A major consideration is the way sexual morality is understood and practiced. This is dealt with first in relation to a particular case of flagrant immorality in the Corinthian church (5:1–13), then more basically with reference to the relationship between sexual morality and freedom (6:12–20).

Presumably basing their position on Paul's teaching about the new free- dom in Christ, some of the church members at Corinth had flaunted a slogan for their new-found liberation: ''I am free to do anything'' (v. 12, repeated in 10:23). Paul qualifies their indiscriminate conception of freedom in two significant ways: Christian freedom means acting ''for the best'' (v. 12a); Christian freedom must not be subverted into another form of enslavement (v. 12b). Freedom, as Paul knows, means to live in the Spirit and for the sake of the community; it is not just a breaking loose from domination by the world, but must also be a new bondage in service to Christ. "All things are yours," yes, but, "you are Christ's; and Christ is God's" (3:22c–23).

Paul deals briefly with the issue of sacrificial foods which will occupy more of his attention in chaps. 8—10. Basically the Corinthian position, "Food is for the stomach and the stomach for food" (v. 13), articulated over against the contention of some for certain food taboos, wins his personal agreement. But on the other issue, that freedom permits not only the cancellation of dietary restrictions but also sexual promiscuity, Paul objects emphatically. He does so, it must be noted, not for hygienic or social welfare reasons, but on Christological grounds. The body (*sōma*) is consecrated not to sexual immorality but to Christ the Lord (v. 13b); it is destined not for destruction, as the external world is, but for resurrection (v. 14; cf. Rom. 8:11).

"Body," for Paul, is a common way of referring to the total self and should be read that way here (note how he uses "body" and "us" in vv. 13 and 14 as equivalent terms). If this is so, he argues, then one cannot belong to another without forfeiting the relationship to Christ. Sexual union with a prostitute is, on the principle of Gen. 2:24, to become "one flesh." That is another way of saying "one body," or even "one spirit," a oneness that must obtain only with the Lord (v. 17). Paul often uses these two words with differentiated meanings; but here they become practically equivalent, both designating an exclusive personal relationship with the Lord.

The image of the believing community as a temple in which the Spirit of God dwells finds expression earlier in this letter (3:16–17) and is one of the ways the Covenanters of Qumran described themselves (1QS ix, 3–6). In the present context Paul individualizes the image and speaks of the true believer as one who is the shrine of the Holy Spirit (v. 19), a correlate of being one spirit with the Lord (v. 17). Being part of the community of Christ—the church—does not mean the denial of individual selfhood. True individuality emerges out of a realization that we are not self-created, self-sustaining, or self-accountable: "You are *not* your own" (v. 19b); you belong to Christ the Lord who gave himself to the uttermost for you, that is, died that you might live (v. 20a). Everything you are, everything you do, therefore, should be an act of praise of God (v. 20b). Only in that understanding of ourselves can we boast, "I am free to do anything," whether with respect to sex or food or anything else.

*Gospel: John 1:43–51.* The episode before us describes the call to discipleship of a model Israelite who is the first in this Gospel to declare the messiahship of Jesus. As gentile priest-astrologers have acknowledged him to be the promised world-deliverer in Matthew's Gospel (2:1–12), so the true Israel, John believes, must recognize him as their King (v. 49).

It is Philip who recruits Nathanael of Cana (21:2), a fellow Galilean, who may have been a follower of John the Baptist. Nathanael is not mentioned by the synoptists in their disciple lists. Some have proposed to identify him with Matthew or Bartholomew, but this is only a conjecture. The Hebrew name means literally "God gives" or "God has given." With John's penchant for symbolism, it is not unreasonable to imagine that the evangelist recognizes in this name the definition of disciples as those whom God has given to Jesus (6:37, and so forth).

Philip tells Nathanael that he and his companions have met the Messiah. The reference to "him of whom Moses in the law . . . wrote" probably alludes to the oracle of Deut. 18:15–19, the "prophet like me." Nathanael's scornful reply, "Can any good thing come out of Nazareth?" is like that of the people in 7:41 and the chief priests in 7:52; it may reflect a popular prejudice against Galilee with its ethnic mixtures and its rabid political messianism. Nathanael is urged to come and see for himself—the first stage of faith (v. 46).

The Jesus of this Gospel has supernatural insight into human thought and ways. He divines immediately according to the Spirit that Nathanael is a model Israelite. If the expression, "when you were under the fig tree" is to be read as a figure for studying Torah, as is a possibility (Eccl. Rab. 5.15), then one is tempted to correlate this description of the true Jew searching the Scriptures with the word of Jesus that it is the very Scriptures that bear witness to him and his mission (John 5:39, 46–47). The outcome of the conversation is the recognition, "Rabbi, you are the son of God! You are the King of Israel!"—both intended to be understood as messianic titles (cf. 12:13 and 2 Sam. 7:14; Ps. 2:7, spoken of the Davidic king).

In reply Jesus promises that a vision will be granted to Nathanael, and presumably the other disciples, of the Son of man in his glory. The allusion in v. 51 is probably to the famous vision of Jacob at Bethel, sanctified by the presence of the holy angels (Gen. 28:12). In the present context John wants his readers to observe that the story of the newest disciple, Nathanael of Cana, will be followed by an incident of a wedding feast in Cana in which the promise given at Nathanael's call is fulfilled: "Jesus . . . manifested his glory; and his disciples believed in him" (2:11). For John that divine glory is not reserved for some eschatological future, as it is by the synoptists, but is manifest here and now in the presence of Christ in the church. Heaven and earth are brought together in Christ.

### HOMILETICAL INTERPRETATION

If it seems that these three texts are not only distant from each other but also from the season of Epiphany, closer examination reveals that that is not the case. Of course, the preacher is free to develop the sermon from one or two of the lections, but it is fruitful to search for common elements that bear upon the theme of Epiphany. All three passages deal with revelation; all three locate that revelation in the house of God; and all three insist on behavior that is appropriate to the house of God.

Before attending to the texts before us, let the mind reflect upon the close tie between worship and conduct in both Judaism and Christianity. It is easy for us to forget that the Bible's insistence upon moral and ethical requirements in the worship of God was voiced in a culture where most religions provided rituals and ceremonies without questioning or making any demand upon the worshiper's life. Judaism called upon those who ascended to Zion to do so with clean hands and pure heart, and the prophets continually called down the judgment of God upon those who sought to make worship services a substitute for ethical uprightness. Such worship was only noise, said the prophets, hated and despised by the Lord. Jesus continued this prophetic witness concerning worship and the moral life. If in the very act of worship, he said, you remember that your brother has something against you, leave your gift at the altar and first be reconciled to the brother. The efficacy of worship is related to the quality of attitude and conduct in the worshiper.

1 Sam. 3:1–20 concerns the house of worship at Shiloh. The aged priest there was Eli, who had a young attendant named Samuel, a boy left there by his mother to serve God. The temple and ritual life had become corrupted by Eli's blaspheming sons; the worship and praise of God in Israel was flickering toward darkness. The house of Eli had to be removed and replaced. God called the boy Samuel, servant to Eli, to pronounce this word of doom. Strange as it may seem, the temple of Shiloh still had within it enough health to nourish this boy to become the voice of self-criticism and judgment. The voice of God was still heard in the temple, even though it spoke a word of judgment. And much to Eli's credit, he accepted that word of judgment upon his house. The story testifies to the power of God to have his word spoken and heard in spite of the decay into which the house of worship had fallen. And the history of the church testifies to this truth again and again. Repeatedly. Whenever and wherever the church has been a moral shambles, with ethically indifferent leaders, someone has arisen to reform and renew it because the voice of God was heard. One does not completely define the church simply by characterizing its members and leaders—there is still God to be reckoned with. Judgment still comes; it begins at the house of God, and there it arrives with greater severity. And why not? Lilies that fester smell worse than weeds.

The temple to be sanctified for the praise of God according to 1 Cor. 6:12–20 is the human body. Such a view of the body was not new for Jews. They thought of the body as an integral part of the self which had been created in God's image. Rabbis would impress this truth upon young minds by taking students to public parks to see the busts of emperors being scrubbed and cleaned. If the stone image of a human ruler is so respected and cared for, how much more respected is the living image of the eternal Holy One. But in Corinth, other views of the body prevailed. Having been reared in a culture that thought dualistically—that is, that body and spirit were from different sources and of different natures—these new Christians had associated Christianity with their spirits but not their bodies. In fact, as a prison of the spirit, the body was best treated indifferently. After all, whether by abuse or by asceticism, the goal was to be free of the body. If, therefore, the body were denied or indulged, what difference did it make in the spirit's salvation? To such minds, gluttony and sexual license were matters of the body and hence of no real consequence. With firm care, Paul tries to explain how the body is a very real factor in defining who we are and what our relationships are. The body is not an arena of indifference; it is a temple of God where the Holy Spirit dwells. Abuses of the body and detached physical relationships are therefore corruptions of the temple.

The body is God's house. The implications of this definition are obvious and many. This is not at all to imply that the Christian life can be characterized as simply good grooming. But on the other hand, neither is it the Christian life to react so negatively to clean-washed piety that self-regard is relinquished in favor of some equally pious claim of self-denial. In the same vein, the bodies of others are to be so regarded. One cannot believe the body is God's temple and refuse attention to those whose bodies are hungry, naked, bruised, or imprisoned. In some circumstances, attending to the physical body of a person is about as "spiritual" as anything one can do.

John 1:43–51 is a brief narrative concluding with a reference to the revelation of God at Bethel (house of God). Nathanael comes to Jesus, but not without first having doubted and questioned. He was an honest and forthright person, neither cynically skeptical nor naively gullible. Jesus commends him even before he believes: an Israelite without guile or deception. Once he is persuaded concerning Jesus, he openly promises Nathanael that an even greater revelation awaits him, one like Jacob's at Bethel: "This is none other than the house of God, and this is the gate of heaven" (Gen. 28:17). Most likely, Nathanael symbolically represents those of Israel who see and hear and come to faith in Jesus. Jesus is the dwelling place of God, the place and manner of God's revelation of himself: "Whoever has seen me has seen God." Jesus is Bethel. But not everyone had an experience like that of Bethel when seeing and hearing Jesus. Why not? If Nathanael is a model here, to sense the presence of God in the presence of Jesus one must be an open and honest seeker, not blinded by guile or deceit. According to John's Gospel, those who will not, cannot.

# The Third Sunday after the Epiphany

| Lutheran | Roman Catholic | Episcopal | Pres/UCC/Chr | Meth/COCU |
|---|---|---|---|---|
| Jon. 3:1–5, 10 | Jon. 3:1–5, 10 | Jer. 3:21—4:2 | Jon. 3:1–5, 10 | Jon. 3:1–5, 10 |
| 1 Cor. 7:29–31 | 1 Cor. 7:29–31 | 1 Cor. 7:17–23 | 1 Cor. 7:29–31 | 1 Cor. 7:29–35 |
| Mark 1:14–20 | Mark 1:14–20 | Mark 1:14–20 | Mark 1:14–20 | Mark 1:14–20 |

## EXEGESIS

*First Lesson: Jon. 3:1–5, 10.* This remarkable critique of prophetism and orthodox notions of covenant and election comes as one of the latest voices of prophecy in Israel. It is estimated to date somewhere between 400 and 200 B.C., in the late Persian or Hellenistic period. It is not intended to be an historical account, but a *mashal*—a parable, with a strong didactic content. In two balanced scenes—Act I: Jonah on the ship (the Prayer of Jonah in chap. 2 is a later addition); Act II: Jonah in Nineveh (3–4)—it tells the story of a stubborn and rebellious prophet who refused the commission to address a foreign nation as a spokesman of Yahweh, only at last to accept it grudgingly, while Jonah remains obstinate to the end in resisting the evidence of divine mercy to penitent Gentiles. Nevertheless God used this disobedient prophet to convert the heathen, to the honor and glory of his name.

The lesson gives us the parable in a nutshell. A second time the divine summons comes to Jonah to go to Nineveh "that great city." The description in 3:2 and the fantastic account of its size in v. 3b, "three days journey in breadth" or 60–75 miles wide, sound like an imaginary account of a fabulous city of a remote time. They exhibit a common feature of parable: heightened effect by calculated extravagance in statement (cf. Jesus' Parable of the Leaven or the Parable of the Unmerciful Servant). This time the reluctant man of God obeyed. Going into the city, the Hebrew prophet cried doom upon the city within forty days.

The message delivered, Jonah retired to see what would happen. To his consternation, the Assyrians repented. The people "believed God," every one of them, just as Abraham was said to have believed God (Gen. 15:6). By their contrition and "turning" they hoped to avert the divine wrath. Pagan Assyrians acknowledge the God of Israel which is to say: Israel's God is Lord of all the peoples of the earth!

The lesson concludes with v. 10. God was moved by their wholehearted penitence and turned himself from the judgment that would have fallen upon them. Scripture elsewhere does not hesitate to speak of a change of mind on God's part (Exod. 32:14; 2 Sam. 24:16; Amos 7:3, 6). His purposes are immutable, but his plans and actions may be altered while they remain directed toward his children's good.

Why is Jonah, this disobedient member of the covenant community, said to be a prophet? Is this, as von Rad proposes, a devastating self-criticism of the prophetic office untrue to its calling, unwilling to act upon the truth of the wideness of God's mercy which it grasps (4:2) but cannot accept (4:3)?

*Second Lesson: 1 Cor. 7:29–31.* Beginning with this seventh chapter in the lengthy letter we call 1 Corinthians, Paul addresses himself to some specific issues raised in a letter from the church at Corinth, brought perhaps by slaves from Chloe's family (1:11). In the portion of the total discussion that constitutes today's lection Paul considers the unmarried state in terms of the Christian's total relationship to the larger world in which he or she is inseparably involved.

Basically Paul counsels detachment from the orders and the business of society, but without separation and withdrawal from it. "As though . . . not" becomes a formula for stating this attitude. Live in this world as though it were not fixed or final. That is, use it, but not completely. Be involved, but not controlled by it. There is no necessity to change one's external status in the social structure (vv. 26–28), but there is no need to be held captive by it either.

In view of this it is best that the married live as though they were unmarried; mourners as though there were no basis for grief; the happy, as though happiness were absent; business carried on as though acquisition were unimportant; life in the world as though one were not preoccupied by it.

There are some interesting parallels to this world-transcending attitude to be found in the writings of Epictetus and Seneca, but for these philosophers it is a matter of attaining *self-sufficiency* by way of indifference to worldly cares and preoccupations: the autonomous life. Paul finds sufficiency or independence not in himself, but only in dependence upon God, letting his own life be ordered by the new world of God's making.

*Gospel: Mark 1:14–20.* For the synoptic evangelists, including Mark, the new time of salvation—which is the message of the gospel—has begun with the pivotal event of John's preaching of baptism, but the fulfillment comes with his successor, Jesus. After John's work had been brought to an end by arrest and imprisonment, Jesus began his work in Galilee. "The time (*kairos*) is fulfilled, and the kingdom of God is at hand; repent, and believe in the gospel" (1:14).

Many metaphors are used in the Gospels to name the new salvation time:

wine, harvest, city, temple, family, banquet, wedding feast; but the metaphor used most frequently by Jesus is "Kingdom of God." What reality does it connote? God as king over all creation, whose sovereignty will finally be established over all his adversaries, is a concept found in the OT (cf. Pss. 45:6; 103:19; 145:11–13; 1 Chr. 29:11; Isa. 52:7). The future has now approached this present world, Jesus declared. An eschatological event is taking place in this present moment, not by a catastrophic destruction of the world, but by an upsetting of everyday human affairs. This world is God's realm, and the eschatological event is God's own act which men and women can seek, receive, inherit, or enter, but cannot make or manipulate.

The story of the call of four disciples (vv. 16–20) is told simply, with a minimum of detail. It is intended by Mark to introduce us to the character of discipleship special to Jesus. Jewish sages and Greek philosophers had their coteries of students just like those who assembled about Jesus of Nazareth. But the differences are significant. Jesus' students are not to become scholars of the Torah, but heralds of God's kingdom. Discipleship calls for unqualified allegiance to Jesus as undisputed master, calls for the life-risking practice of unconditional love and obedience to what God is doing now through this teacher. It is, in fact, a wholly new kind of existence in the present in view of an imminent future.

Jesus enlists four fishermen: Simon and Andrew, James and John. They join him immediately. Mark shows us what discipleship requires: resolute action, full response, risk—and no returning.

### HOMILETICAL INTERPRETATION

Epiphany, the manifestation of our Lord, was an event with place and time. Christians insist that calendars, therefore, should reflect it, historians record it. Admittedly, there have been problems of precision as to time of year; in fact, even the exact year is not universally agreed upon. But no matter; that Christ's appearance was an important event in world history was not to be overlooked. Luke especially wanted the fact of the coming of Christ entered into the record. He dated it by listing who at the time was emperor of Rome, who ruled Judea and Galilee, and who was high priest (Luke 3:1–2). And the Christian world, by restructuring its calendar and marking events with B.C. and A.D., has said that Christ's coming was *the* time.

It is not, of course, unimportant to have our records and calendars bear witness to our faith. The event of Epiphany was history and history-changing. But excessive attention to this dimension of Christ's appearance can cause us to overlook several important truths to which Scripture witnesses.

First, while historical time, *chronos* (the word from which we get *chronology*), is very important to the Bible's narrative about what God is doing as he unfolds his purpose for the world, the Scriptures also reflect a concern for another kind of time. This kind of time is called *kairos*. The word refers not to time that is marked by clocks and calendars, but to those times that are special, those times that are unusually opportune. We sometimes signal such a time as "our time" or "our moment." In John's Gospel, Jesus spoke and acted not according to pressures or demands, but according to his sense of the *kairos:* "My hour has come." The Scriptures understand *kairos* to testify to the conviction that not only in and through, but beyond the events of calendar time, God is at work to bring about a special intersection of factors so as to create *the* hour, *the* moment. These moments, these events, are God-given, and when they occur, life changes, history changes. In fact, these times are of such significance that those who grasp their importance look upon their *chronos*, their calendars in a new way. Past and future receive a new interpretation. Epiphany was not just *chronos;* it was *kairos*.

Second, Christians should not think solely of the Christ event as the time of God's redeeming activity. The Scriptures testify repeatedly to moments of God's closing one time and beginning a new time for his people. If we may think of these occasions as characterized by ending and beginning, old and new, death and resurrection, judgment and grace, then the mind is flooded with them. God made clothes for Eden's guilty pair, preserved Noah and his family, brought Israel home from exile, and on and on. God's time always meant a new day for his people.

Such was Nineveh's experience in our text from the Book of Jonah. For wickedness Nineveh was notorious. That wickedness combined with the fact that these people were non-Jews, convinced Jonah that at least in this case God's act would not be judgment and grace, but judgment only. After a slow start Jonah was able to generate enthusiasm for a rousing sermon on God's wrath against sinners. As he started the countdown to destruction, he should have grown suspicious of the outcome when he saw city-wide repentance. God accepts the penitent who truly turn from sin. And so, in one of the Bible's strange but beautiful expressions, "God repents" and spares the city. Jonah's earlier reservations about preaching to those Assyrians find confirmation and he is quick to tell the Almighty: "This is the very reason I ran from this job in the first place, 'for I knew that thou art a gracious God and merciful, slow to anger, and abounding in steadfast love, and repentest of evil' " (4:2). It is too bad that Jonah resisted a truth he knew from the start: God's time is not just end time, not just judgment time, but always an opportunity for a beginning, a new day. There is no condition so empty of hope, so depraved, so deprived, so distant from God, that mourning cannot be turned into joy.

However, the joy in Nineveh is muted by the obstinate resistance of Jonah. He cannot enter into that joy. After all, God has accepted persons who, in Jonah's calculations, should not be embraced. But in this dark mood Jonah is not alone. This is the fundamental problem humans have with God—not that he is cruel or vengeful, but that he is gracious. It is not so much his treatment of us that grates, but his generosity toward others. Who among us has not felt that we keep better records on human behavior than God does? Who among us has not been offended by a gracious God who pays full wage to one-hour workers, who is kind to the ungrateful and selfish, who sends sun and rain on the just and the unjust, and who gives parties for prodigals? God's offer of a new time destroys our sense of righteousness, but fulfills his own.

A third truth overlooked by those who think of the Christ event solely in historical terms has to do with the believer's personal experience of God's *kairos*. To think of Christ's coming as historically future is not erroneous but inadequate. Of course, Scriptures testify to a past and future in chronological sequence but they also amply refer to past and future as experienced in the present. The end of one age overlapping the beginning of another is one way to characterize the life of faith. Such a description is a major contribution of Paul's theology. While he never abandoned his belief in an end of all things as they now are, he repeatedly described the Christian life as the experience of the old having passed away and the new having begun. His language on the topic varied: death and resurrection, old and new creation, Adam and Christ; but there is never any doubt about his meaning. Coming to faith is an experience of God's time, the end and the beginning now.

In this way Paul describes for the Corinthians the life style of the new age. To live in the world and in all our relationships "as though . . . not" cannot be understood literally; such life would not be freedom but irresponsibility. But Paul does mean that for those whose confidence is in God, the old has passed away. All values, involvements, and relationships have been reinterpreted. Old preoccupations, when they reach the point of absolutizing and idolizing, have been broken. Things, relationships, gains, and losses are all seen for what they are: values, but only relative, transient values. To be under the control and determination of these values is the nature of life in the old era. But now a new time has been granted us, and the nature of the new is freedom.

As one reads 1 Cor. 7:29–31, the freedom of which Paul speaks may seem to be a kind of indifference to the world and its claims, but it only *seems* so. In fact, in this new freedom one can work and share and relate more meaningfully than ever because the clutching, grasping, clamoring, "I must have it or I will die" anxiety is gone. As Paul wrote to his friends at Philippi, "whether I come or not, whether I am in prison or not, whether I have much or little, these are not the main thing. Rather, I keep both hands free to lay hold of him who laid hold of me." Although Paul rarely uses the word "repentance," all that the word conveys is expressed here. God's time intersects one's life; it is Nineveh again, and Jonah is preaching. In God's grace, the old has passed away and the new has come.

Finally, those who think of the event of Christ's coming as the central moment in history often fail to move inside the Christ event to see and hear what he actually was doing and saying. For many Christians, the whole of the gospel is swiftly gathered up in the death and resurrection of Jesus. But in the NT the church has preserved accounts of what Jesus said and did. This, too, is important. And what did Jesus do and say? In our Gospel for today Mark summarizes that ministry: Jesus came into Galilee, preaching the gospel of God, and saying, The time is fulfilled, and the kingdom of God is at hand; repent and believe in the gospel. Now, says Jesus, is the *kairos*, God's time; the heavens have been split and a new age now dawns. If one turns from the old in repentance one can participate in God's reign, God's kingdom. Those who hear and follow find the new radically new. They leave everything and become fishers of men. Life for them is never the same. The old has been stripped away and they stand before the new, naked, quivering, afraid, ecstatic, trusting.

As one reads Mark's sharp, uncompromising lines, the meaning is clear. It is Nineveh again, but one greater than Jonah is here.

# The Fourth Sunday after the Epiphany

| Lutheran | Roman Catholic | Episcopal | Pres/UCC/Chr | Meth/COCU |
|---|---|---|---|---|
| Deut. 18:15–20 | Deut. 18:15–20 | Deut. 18:15–20 | Deut. 18:15–22 | Deut. 18:15–22 |
| 1 Cor. 8:1–13 | 1 Cor. 7:32–35 | 1 Cor. 8:1b–13 | 1 Cor. 7:32–35 | 1 Cor. 8:1–13 |
| Mark 1:21–28 | Mark 1:21–28 | Mark 1:21–28 | Mark 1:21–28 | Mark 1:21–28 |

## EXEGESIS

*First Lesson: Deut. 18:15–20.* In the discussion of the lection from John's Gospel (1:43–51) for the Second Sunday after Epiphany, we had occasion to speak of the Jewish expectation of the Mosaic eschatological prophet. This Sunday's OT lesson contains the passage in the Torah which John had in mind.

There is no question that Moses is the decisive figure in the Pentateuch, from the events of the Exodus from Egypt through the wanderings in the wilderness and the final arrival at the promised land. To the Deuteronomist he is seen as the chief of the prophets, proclaiming to Israel the word of Yahweh (Deut. 18:18). He is the true and only mediator between Israel and Yahweh, the one who suffers vicariously for the people, making intercession for them (Deut. 9:18ff., 25ff.), the meek and obedient servant of God (Deut. 3:24; 34:5).

In the verses before us, God is to raise up a mediator-prophet in the future who will command the obedience of Israel (v. 15). This future prophet will be like the true prophet, Moses, who was appointed at Sinai, at the request of the people, as a representative who would stand for them in the divine presence and hear what God wanted to say to his people (vv. 16–17; cf. 5:23–27). The early church found in this scripture a promise fulfilled in the person of Jesus Christ. In the christology of early Jewish Christianity, "Prophet" became the principal title for the Messiah, Jesus.

In what follows in the lesson, we hear the testimony of experience dealing with confused and conflicting prophetic claims. The Deuteronomist proposes a simple, oft-repeated, but tenuous criterion: If the word comes to pass, it is authentic; if not, it is counterfeit (v. 22). He knows that verification, in the final analysis, is not verbal (shout louder!) but experimental (does it work?). Revelation claims must be tested in the crucible of human experience if they are to be believed as a disclosure of truth.

*Second Lesson: 1 Cor. 8:1–13.* Last week's lection, from 1 Corinthians 7, dealt with sexual immorality. A second item on the agenda presented to Paul by the Corinthian church concerned the matter of eating meat that might have been offered as a sacrifice to the city's guardian deities. Confronting this particular issue, Paul is able to define some aspects of his understanding of freedom and responsibility that reach far beyond the local situation. There were obviously some members of the church who represented a liberal position with a gnostic flavor, arguing their right (*exousia*) to participate in pagan sacramental meals and to share table hospitality with pagan families. Others, more conservative, were confused by this conduct, either strenuously rejecting it or foolishly following suit while troubled in mind for doing so.

Some clues to the thinking of the Corinthian liberals are furnished in Paul's restatement of their arguments: "All of us possess knowledge"; "An idol has no real existence" (v. 4a); "There is no God but one" (v. 4b); "All things are lawful for me" (6:12; 10:23). Basically Paul agrees with them; meat offered to the gods is not harmful in itself and can be eaten by the believer. But he is convinced that the problem is deeper than issues of diet and courtesy. Their vaunted knowledge is far from being mature (v. 2). Knowledge *(gnosis)*, as they are experiencing it, results in a false sense of sufficiency; it is an ego trip. It is concerned with personal rights and privileges and insists on dominating everything and everyone (vv. 1b, 9, 11). By contrast, the concern of love *(agapē)* is for the other person, subordinating individual rights to the needs of others. Conduct is tested in terms of whether it enhances or destroys community. Notice in v. 3 the way Paul changes the outcome of the conditional clause "If one loves God." It is not what the reader expects it to be: "one will then know God." Instead the consequence is, *"one is known by God"* (1 Cor. 13:12; Gal. 4:9). Not to lay claim to a knowledge of God (as the Corinthians may be boasting), but to be known—that is, chosen, elected by God—that is what really matters.

Paul can affirm with the liberal Corinthians a monotheistic faith that does not admit the real existence of other divine beings. He recognizes only one God who is Father—who is Source ("from whom are all things") and End ("for whom we exist"), and one Lord Jesus Christ—who is Mediator of creation ("through whom are all things") and human existence ("through whom we exist," v. 6). He uses a very early bipartite credal formula to dethrone all other supernatural powers.

Be that as it may, the fact is that at Corinth not everyone has fully understood this. Paul reminds the liberals that there are weaker members of the community who believe that these other gods really do exist, and that for them therefore eating sacrificial meat violates an undivided loyalty to the one and only God. What for one can be an acknowledgement that God alone is Lord, for another becomes an act of infidelity (v. 7). Thus by one's assertion of freedom, another is destroyed (v. 11). One man's meat . . .

For knowledge to be exercised in love, therefore, means that liberation must be expressed responsibly in a way that accepts responsibility for the well-being of others. Paul understands sin to be a violation of the needs of the brother or sister, and because Christ presents himself in the person of the other, such a violation is a sin against Christ himself (vv. 11–12). The rights *(exousiai)* of others are to take priority over one's own. That's a new and disturbing reading of human rights!

*Gospel: Mark 1:21–28.* Mark moves abruptly from the story of the call of the first disciples to an episode in the Capernaum synagogue on a Sabbath day in which Jesus teaches and performs a healing. Capernaum *(Kefar Nahum)*, an important town on the north western shores of the Galilee lake, becomes in the synoptics a base for Jesus' work in the district. The interest of the evangelist is in the cure as a demonstration of the authority *(exousia)* of Jesus' teaching.

A sick man who heard Jesus speak burst out, "What do you have against us?" That is to say, the spirit plaguing him recognized in the person of Jesus one who was no friend, but a foe. Just so was Elijah challenged by the widow of Zarephath when she was grieving over her dead son (1 Kings 17:18). The sick man—or rather the evil spirit—addresses Jesus as the Holy One of God, a rarely used title, unknown as a messianic title in Judaism. It is found again in John 6:69 in the messianic confession of Peter, "You are the Holy One of God."

Using no incantation or magical potions according to the fashion of other Jewish and Greek exorcists of the day, Jesus addresses the unclean spirit with a commanding word, "Be quiet (literally, *muzzled*) and come out of him!" (v. 25). In a final paroxysm, the sick man screams and suddenly finds relief. The storyteller's comment is to be noted. Jesus' power over the evil spirits, demonstrated in this extraordinary healing, is an exhibition of the authority of his teaching (v. 27).

Behind the ancient form of this healing story, we can recognize an intuitive understanding of illness as alien to the will of God. This is the kingdom beginning to happen. Its new life appears wherever Jesus is present, as Mark and his congregation can testify.

## HOMILETICAL INTERPRETATION

The lections for today may seem to be gold nuggets lying on the ground, available without digging. Since Epiphany celebrates the manifestation of Christ, all three texts join without struggle in that celebration. A christocentric message can be informed and nourished not solely by Mark's story of Jesus working powerfully in a synagogue in Capernaum but by Deuteronomy and 1 Corinthians as well. Deut. 18:15–20 provided the early church with a central image and prophecy of the Christ. Jesus, said the early Christians, is the one of whom Moses spoke, the prophet whom God raised up as he had raised up Moses (Acts 3:22–23). Deut. 18:15–20 may have been the basis for Matthew's portrait of Jesus as Moses-like: among the rich and powerful in infancy, saved from a tyrant's slaughter of children, called out of Egypt, and bringing the word of God from the mountain. In many ways, the early church understood this passage from Deuteronomy to be fulfilled in Jesus Christ. And 1 Cor. 8:1–13, while it discusses an apparently minor and distant problem of eating practices in Corinth, contains in v. 6 an early Christian confession of faith in God as creator and end of life, and faith in Jesus Christ as the agent of creation and redemption. And so, without exegetical gymnastics, the preacher welcomes these texts as they intersect in the person of Christ. The sermon thus born and informed would not be without real merit.

However, it is possible to be seduced by the texts that offer their meanings so easily. Behind and beneath terms and titles that have christological import lie the discussions taking place in these three lections. Within these discussions, each with its own context and integrity, one hears a message central to the meaning of Epiphany: The appearance of our Lord brings into the world an authoritative word from God.

Deuteronomy is a sermon that brings forward the Exodus tradition for a new day. As Moses had been the spokesman for God in his day, the people sought another who would continue to bring the word from God. They did not wish to be brought near the awesome and terrifying Presence, but they wanted the word of God from someone who was near the Presence and who, therefore, could speak with authority. In response to this expressed need, God promised to raise up another like Moses, a prophet who would take the message from God and deliver it to the people.

One question, however, haunted the promise. How will we know if the one who claims to speak God's word is truly a prophet? Israel knew, as the church was later to know, that "Thus saith the Lord" is shouted from every street corner; and the several messengers often do not agree with each other. The answer given by Deuteronomy may not be fully satisfying but it is straightforward: If the message does not happen, does not come true, then the prophet was false (18:20–22).

This text has raised the thorny issue with which the community of faith has always had to struggle, and from that struggle no full relief has yet come. The question remains the same: How can we know if the word proclaimed is from God? Deut. 18:15–20 is concerned about this problem from two sides. On the one hand, there are those who do not speak what they have heard (18:19). For what reasons are they silent? Perhaps cowardice, perhaps fear of loss of income or position or life, perhaps indifference. On the other hand, there are those who speak what they have not heard. From them the people of God have sought to protect themselves with criteria for discerning the truth. These criteria have been moral, ethical, doctrinal, organizational, and (at times) political, but never in history has there been full guarantee against putting truth on the scaffold and error on the throne.

The church at Corinth was in search of the Word among all the words. Messengers were sent to Paul with reports of discord, and a letter was sent to him asking for clarification on issues about Christian living, public worship, and matters of belief (1 Cor. 7:1). One of those issues, whether to eat meat sacrificed to idols, is the concern of today's Second Lesson. Some in the congregation at Corinth seem to have the word. Among their slogans are: "An idol has no real existence" and "All of us possess knowledge" and "There is no god but one." These slogans seem true enough, so what is the problem? The problem is this: Being right or even saying what is true is not enough. In fact, under some circumstances it could even be divisive and harmful. Knowledge alone is not the creator of the fellowship, but love—concern for the condition of another, restraint upon one's own rights in regard for the rights of others. This is the word for the church, says Paul, for

one criterion by which one judges if the words spoken are the word of God
is whether or not the words build up, edify, the body of Christ.

It is important to notice, however, that Paul does not wish to argue with
those who have filled the air with slogans of truth. That would add more
words and could easily degenerate into a game of who has the best slogan.
Instead, Paul quotes the confession of faith which they know and had used,
perhaps at their baptism. "There is one God, the Father, from whom are all
things and for whom we exist, and one Lord, Jesus Christ, through whom
are all things and through whom we exist" (8:6).

In Mark 1:21–28, the word is on the lips of Jesus. Mark often refers to
Jesus as teacher and to his words as teaching; Mark's concern, however, is
not so much to detail the content of that teaching as to focus upon its power.
To highlight this power, Mark sketches a scene in a synagogue. The scene
opens with Jesus teaching and closes with the crowd amazed at his teaching. Sandwiched between is not a discussion of what Jesus said but an
account of an exorcism. Apparently Mark relates the exorcism in order to
illustrate the power of Jesus' word. And so it does. The word of Jesus is
addressed to the evil spirit which has possessed a man. The evil spirit
screams words at Jesus and the battle is on. What the evil spirit says is true:
Jesus *is* the Holy One of God. But a demon speaking the truth is still a
demon. Jesus hurls his words at the demon and the demon's power over the
man is broken.

In this case, what is the word among these words? It is interesting that the
evil spirit spoke the truth; in fact, the demon acknowledged Jesus as the
Holy One of God. The scene is reminiscent of the devil quoting Scripture in
tempting Jesus (Matt. 4:6). But in these verbal battles it is the word on
Jesus' lips that is the word of God. And by what criterion? Immediately, of
course, one thinks of the criterion of character: the Son of God versus a
spirit of evil. However, some may be hesitant to generalize the occasion
into a principle: It is the quality of the speaker's life that makes the words
Word of God. Another criterion is the character of God: Ours is a God who
loves and cares for people, who seeks their wholeness and health, who
speaks healing rather than harming words. The evil spirit possesses, alien-
ates, and cripples physically, socially, mentally, and spiritually, as the NT
frequently characterizes the work of demonic powers. One might conclude, then, that words which cripple human life, even though what is
spoken contains Scripture verses and Christian vocabulary, are not word
of God.

A modern reader may be surprised that the arsenal from which Jesus
drew his weapons for battling against evil contained words. We think of
other means of combating evil in our society; for many, words have come to
mean little and to contain even less power. Deeds, not words, we say. But
such was not the case in biblical literature. In Scripture, creation is by the

word, redemption is by the word, and judgment is by the word. There is in the Bible no power to equal that described in the expression "And God said." For Christians, the central act of God is captured in the expression, "The Word became flesh." Words *are* deeds. And for all the glut of words in our day, the rape of our language, the demonic uses of communication, nevertheless, speaking and hearing remain fundamental human acts. They also remain the most difficult, for while we may chatter easily, we draw our breath in pain to communicate about matters of ultimate concern. It is as though the mind and body know instinctively that to speak is to break the silence, to give one's word, to participate in the ceaseless battle between good and evil.

Among other things, Epiphany means, "and God said."

## The Fifth Sunday after the Epiphany

| Lutheran | Roman Catholic | Episcopal | Pres/UCC/Chr | Meth/COCU |
|---|---|---|---|---|
| Job 7:1–7 | Job 7:1–4, 6–7 | 2 Kings 4:(8–17) 18–21 (22–31) 32–37 | Job 7:1–7 | Job 7:1–7 |
| 1 Cor. 9:16–23 | 1 Cor. 9:16–19, 22–23 | 1 Cor. 9:16–23 | 1 Cor. 9:16–19, 22–23 | 1 Cor. 9:16–23 |
| Mark 1:29–39 | Mark 1:29–39 | Mark 1:29–39 | Mark 1:29–39 | Mark 1:29–39 |

### EXEGESIS

*First Lesson: Job 7:1–7.* It is generally recognized that the prose framework of the Book of Job (1—2; 42:7–17) is a very old story, certainly dating from the preexilic period. It told of a Hebrew man who, amidst tribulation, remained loyal and obedient to God and who gained recompense for his faithfulness. Into this naive story of goodness rewarded a Jewish poet of the late Persian or early Hellenistic period inserted a lengthy poetic dialogue. Here we see no confident, trusting Job, but a man who, driven to the depths of misery by God's own doing, nonetheless protests his own innocence to the end.

It is this stubborn insistence on his own righteousness that is the subject of Job's contention with God (chap. 31). Job reflects the traditional view that every human act carries with it consequences that are inescapable, and this totality of action and result must be assigned to the supreme will of the Creator God. Job revoices this traditional explanation, but he cannot accept it, because he believes a punishment has fallen upon him where no wrong has been committed.

The passage chosen for today's lesson is a refrain frequently echoed in this book, a melancholy reminder of the burdensome quality of human existence. It is a realistic and candid account of what Koheleth describes as "Vanity of vanities" (Eccles. 1:2) and another poet, "If after all that we have lived and thought, all comes to naught, . . . why live?" (E. A. Robinson). "Months of emptiness," "nights of misery" are the unhappy lot of this wretched man. He sees his lifetime slipping away from him and at its end he knows there is no hope (v. 6). Here Job shares the common conviction of his people that there is no life after death, only an endless sleep in Sheol (14:12–14). Only in later Judaism are there the first signs of a hope for conscious survival in an awakening from the sleep of death.

In sum, life is a breath, insubstantial and brief (cf. Ps. 78:39, "a wind that passes and comes not again"; Eccles. 1:14). Life is ephemeral, dismal, and wracked with pain. Such is suffering Job's conclusion.

*Second Lesson: 1 Cor. 9:16–23.* This discussion of the right of an apostle to material support from the congregation is set in the context of rights and privileges bearing upon the troublesome matter of idol sacrifices and the Christian conscience. It may be that in this discussion of ritual sacrifices, Paul takes the opportunity to reply pointedly to some of his critics. They insinuate that his practice of self-support is a tacit admission of his being inferior to the true apostles, who in their teaching and preaching accept without questions the largess of the community (9:5–6). It is as if the liberals' claim to a "right" to eat and drink whatever they wished reminds him of another application of that freedom, namely his own "right"—no less than that of the other apostolic missionaries—to bed and board from the community he is serving.

After asserting uncompromisingly that he and the other apostles, on scriptural (v. 9) and dominical (v. 14) authority, have the right (*exousia*) to support, he faces the criticism that he does not accept it. To his critics this refusal invalidates his claim to apostleship. This point he denies categorically. He has voluntarily renounced his apostolic rights to their support (v. 15a). He preaches the gospel not as a personal achievement but as a holy responsibility (v. 16). If it were his own doing, he could take satisfaction in it and expect a reward (*misthos,* pay; v. 17a). But he is constrained to do what he does. And his reward? His boast is that he has no ground for boasting! (vv. 15b, 16). His reward is that he makes no claims upon the gospel he preaches! (v. 18).

The material included in this lection is closely allied to the issue of conscience, freedom, and responsibility begun in 8:1. Paul chooses to speak here of "freedom" rather than "right," the watchwords preferred by the Corinthian liberals, and argues his understanding of freedom as voluntary submission to the service of others.

The expression "under the law of Christ" (v. 21) sounds strange on the lips of this man who taught that Christ is the end of the law (Rom. 10:4). We must exercise great care in defining Paul's attitude toward the law, recognizing that he employs the word in several ways. Perhaps here we are to understand the law of Christ as the twofold law of love, remembered as the summary of Christ's teaching and life by the early church (Mark 12:28–34 and parallels).

With specific reference to the Corinthian situation (see 8:13) Paul continues his explanation that true freedom does not mean specific privilege but service (cf. Mark 10:43ff.; Luke 22:25ff.). "I have identified with the weak. I have become all things to all men" (v. 22). The apparently self-serving motive he attributes to this kind of conduct (v. 23) must be heard in terms of his repeated efforts to become a paradigm for others (2 Cor. 1:14; 1 Thess. 1:6; 1 Cor. 4:16; 11:1).

*Gospel: Mark 1:29–39.* Mark's account continues with the healing of Peter's mother-in-law (vv. 29–31), a summary statement of healings (vv. 32–34), and a departure from Capernaum (vv. 35–38).

The story of the healing of Peter's mother-in-law stands in contrast to the previous synagogue healing. No word is spoken; the sick woman responds to Jesus' helping hand, rises from her bed, and feels well and strong. Mark wants us to observe in the conclusion "she served them" that the authority of Jesus is again demonstrated in action; and discipleship, which should follow, is expressed in specific acts of service.

"All" in the sense of "many" (v. 32; cf. v. 34) sick people were carried to the house of Peter, and Jesus healed them. It may be that Mark distinguished between sickness and demon possession, both of which are amenable to Jesus' curative power (vv. 32–34), but in view of the fact that illness of every sort was at that time attributed to demonic power it seems doubtful that a distinction can be maintained.

How are we to understand the injunction to silence (in v. 25 and again in v. 34), building up to what becomes a refrain in this Gospel? The demons are not permitted to speak because they have supernatural discernment of Jesus' true identity as the Messiah, an identity he does not want disclosed. "He would not permit the demons to speak, because they knew him." (v. 34; cf. 3:12). Nor does Jesus permit those released from the control of evil powers to advertise their cure (1:44; 5:43; 7:36; 8:26). Manifestly the request was impossible to keep. Why the persistent command, consistently violated?

It becomes clear to us that this is the evangelist's rewriting of the older stories that have come to him. His own conviction is that the full disclosure of Jesus' identity as the Son of God was made in the climactic events of the cross and resurrection. The occasional breaching of the concealed truth before that final revelation at the end serves to preview the final events of disclosure which set into motion "the gospel of Jesus Christ, the Son of God." The writer's dramatic skill gives expression to his theological insight.

### HOMILETICAL INTERPRETATION

The readings for today call upon the worshipers and the preacher to reflect on the meaning of Epiphany in the context of conditions not of one's own choosing or liking. It is a fact common to the human lot that many strong factors affecting one's life are not a matter of one's own choices. There are decisions made for us, not only in our childhood but throughout life, over which we have no control. In addition, there are conditions which, though never a matter of one's own decision, are nevertheless determinative: race, skin color, sex, general physical condition, level of intelligence, family group, and all the circumstances attendant upon the time and place of birth. And beyond all this, it has been the belief of many that there lie powers above and beyond us that shape our destinies, perhaps even before we are born. These powers have been called Fate, Chance, Fortune, Destiny, or Stars, and reference to these powers has served as a way to penetrate the mystery surrounding human life. "She leads a charmed life," they said. Some have been so persuaded that life is totally determined that they conclude there is no freedom; whoever thinks he or she is making a decision is entertaining an illusion. So profoundly did such views grip many ancient people that they went to places such as Delphi, in Greece to have a priest or priestess give them a reading of their fate. Will we ever have children? Will the child be healthy? Will our army win the battle? Will my husband return from war? In a perhaps less religious but definitely serious vein many people today go to certain persons for readings; their sober brows scan palms, tea leaves, crystal balls, and the stars. In response to such readings, ancient and modern, some people have wept, some leaped for joy, and some shaken their fists at heaven.

When one reflects on how belief in God as creator and provider affects one's interpretation of the conditions of life, the first response is one of relief, gratitude, and freedom. We are not miniscule parts in a cosmic machine, grinding its unalterable way. We are created in God's image, objects of divine love and care, partners in the business of recreating and reconciling the world. But on another level, belief in God so intensifies the problem of understanding life, especially in times of anguish, as to defy interpretation. With a God who creates and lovingly sustains, how am I to understand my pain and tragedy? The lections for today offer different responses to "heaven's hand."

As our exegete has informed us, the Book of Job is an old story that has apparently undergone revisions, weaving what may have begun as a relatively simple discussion of reward and punishment into a complex drama probing the problem of human suffering. Is there, as Job's friends argue, a direct correlation between one's conduct and one's circumstances in life? Does divine logic permit one to look upon the poor, the crippled, the oppressed and ask, "What sin have you committed?"? Or, conversely, to look upon the healthy and wealthy and say, "Blessed are you who have found favor in God's sight."? In a variety of forms, the question painfully erupts in both the Old and New Testament. Psalm 1 affirms that the righteous are like a tree by a stream; everything they do prospers while the wicked predictably fail. On the other hand, Psalm 73 complains of the prosperity of the wicked in contrast to the poverty of the upright. When the tower of Siloam fell and killed eighteen, why did it kill those particular persons? Were they worse sinners than others? No, said Jesus (Luke 13:1–5). Jesus' disciples looked upon a man blind from birth and asked Jesus, "Who sinned?" (John 9:2). Some observers at the cross, witnessing Jesus' suffering and death, took the fact that God did not intervene and rescue him as proof positive that Jesus was a sinner. This same question is pursued in some of the greatest literature of our civilization. Recall, for example, Thornton Wilder's *The Bridge of San Luis Rey*. Is the misery of a person's life to be explained always as God's punishment for flawed behavior?

Job said no. Job refused to accept that his miserable state had its roots within himself. As he reflects on his condition, his moods range from melancholy to protesting anger. And Job is not the only OT character to stand toe to toe with the Almighty. Moses and many of the prophets reasoned and argued and questioned in a vigorously healthy relationship with God. That relationship, rather than proofs and answers, was primary. It grew stronger by each exercise. Of course, they did not come away from those wrestling matches with answers to the mysteries that are tucked away in God's own counsel, but they came away with the blessing. It is in many ways regrettable that Christians have defined faith in such passive terms and have made devotion such a submissive act. Some would find a vigorous engagement with the Almighty absolutely impossible. If done in a time of great distress, even greater distress and feelings of guilt would follow. Perhaps we should let the OT give us permission to be open and honest with God. Certainly God can handle himself for a few rounds anyway, and we might gain something in losing. Those who have carefully charted the path that the human spirit takes through grief have taught us of the health in honest protest to God.

Paul offers us in 1 Cor. 9:16–23 a different view of heaven's hand in human affairs. The issue is not suffering but freedom. Those in the Corinthian church who define freedom as the full exercise of one's rights cannot understand Paul's restraints upon his own rights in the service of other principles and values. Paul's refusal to accept pay for his services, pay to which he was fully entitled, gets for him not praise but criticism. He is probably not really an apostle, they said. Paul writes in defense of his rights and then explains his refusal to claim them. He said he did not choose this life for himself; preaching was not a profession which he voluntarily embraced. Rather than choosing, he was chosen; rather than volunteering, necessity was laid upon him.

Our present concern is not with the intricacies of Paul's argument but with his use of the word "necessity" to describe his life in ministry. The word is not to be understood psychologically, as though he desired so strongly to preach that he "just had to." Rather the word translated "necessity," *anangkē,* can be translated "fate" or "destiny." In pagan culture it referred to one's having been chosen by the gods for a certain role or a specific destiny. To observers, such persons seemed driven or obsessed or compelled. They could do nothing else. Paul uses this powerful image to describe the hand of God laid upon his life. No doubt he refers in particular to his experience near Damascus. Elsewhere he said he had been set apart from his mother's womb (Gal. 1:15).

When a person senses the hand of heaven so strongly that it can be called "necessity," is that person free? Can such a person be free? Paul says absolutely, yes. Such a person is of course not free in the sense of sauntering through life sampling attractive options. But who says that is freedom? Freedom seems to be dialectically related to constraint, necessity. Some of our greatest documents on human freedom have been written in prison when all the locomotions of apparent freedom have been stopped. Perhaps Paul's "necessity" functioned this way for him. Paul embraced necessity; he laid hold of that which had laid hold of him. Thus freed of all other claims upon his life, he was able to take hold of his destiny with both hands. Acting in that freedom, he demonstrated that he had no need whatsoever to prove he was free. "For though I am free from all men, I have made myself a slave to all, that I might win the more" (1 Cor. 9:19).

In comparison to the two preceding texts, the Gospel for today seems simple indeed. Mark 1:29–39 speaks of persons who are ill, but there is no railing against heaven for woes undeserved, no philosophical musing over the mystery of life's inequities. This text speaks of persons whose lives have been impacted upon by supernatural powers, but there is no evidence that any of these persons had the ability or appetite to theologize about fate and the freedom that comes with the embrace of necessity. The plain truth is, these people are sick and they want to be well. They have heard of the healing and exorcising power of Jesus, and so they come to him in large numbers. From Jesus' standpoint, much more is involved than being sick and being healed. What that "much more" is lies beyond the crowd's—or even his disciples'—understanding, and so he asks everyone to keep quiet and not broadcast his healings. When Golgotha comes, the truth about him and his work will be known.

In the meantime, these folk have no mind for the ultimate ends of being and the final meaning of things. This is not a seminary; this is Galilee and taxes are high, pay is low, life is hard, we are sick, and demons are everywhere. Jesus, can you help? And he does. Is that too simple?

# The Sixth Sunday after the Epiphany

| Lutheran | Roman Catholic | Episcopal | Pres/UCC/Chr | Meth/COCU |
|----------|----------------|-----------|--------------|-----------|
| 2 Kings 5:1–14 | Lev. 13:1–2, 44–46 | 2 Kings 5:1–15b | Lev. 13:1–2, 44–46 | 2 Kings 5:1–15b or Lev. 13:1–2, 44–46 |
| 1 Cor. 9:24–27 | 1 Cor. 10:31—11:1 | 1 Cor. 9:24–27 | 1 Cor. 10:31—11:1 | 1 Cor. 9:24–27; 10:31—11:1 |
| Mark 1:40–45 | Mark 1:40–45 | Mark 1:40–45 | Mark 1:40–45 | Mark 1:40–45 |

## EXEGESIS

*First Lesson: 2 Kings 5:1–15b.* The OT lesson for this day is an excerpt from a series of wonder stories about two ninth-century prophets, Elijah and Elisha, found in the history of the kings (1 Kings 17—2 Kings 13:20). The present story of Naaman the Syrian who was cured of his leprosy by Elisha is one of them.

Naaman was a military commander in the army of an unidentified king of Syria. He learns from a Hebrew female slave that a prophet in Samaria, one of her people, can cure him of his leprosy. The Syrian king sends Naaman to the king of Israel with a letter asking that the king cure Naaman's leprosy. The king of Israel suspects the request to be an act of provocation, since he admits complete helplessness to comply: "Am I God, to kill and to make alive?" (v. 7). Elisha's response is to ask that the Syrian be sent to him in order that each Israelite and Syrian, king and commander, may know that in Israel there is an authentic prophet who is able to do what he says, that is, utter an effective word in the name of the Lord.

When Naaman arrives in Israel he is offended that the prophet Elisha refuses to give him an audience and speak a word of exorcism. Furthermore, Naaman takes umbrage at the prophet's command to bathe in the Jordan, a muddy stream compared to the beautiful rivers of Damascus, his homeland. Prevailed upon by his servants to obey the order, however strange, Naaman does so and experiences a miraculous healing.

Returning to Elisha, the man of God, Naaman makes this confession: "Behold, I know that there is no God in all the earth but in Israel, . . ." (v. 15). This remarkable acknowledgement, together with the observation in v. 1 that it was Yahweh who made possible Naaman's military victories for Syria, has led one scholar to insist on an eighth-century date for the story, since Amos 9:7 is the earliest claim that Israel's God governs the nations of the world. The sequel, however, shows that Naaman continues to think in terms of Baalism, when he requests "two mules' burden of earth" to take home with him. The Syrian was not the last to confuse the one God of all the world with a tribal deity who can be worshiped only on the soil of the Israelite!

*Second Lesson: 2 Cor. 9:24–27.* The illustration continues of Paul's personal renunciation of the rights and privileges attendant upon the apostolic office. In some ways the image of Paul the athlete seems ill-suited to the argument that is being set out in chaps. 8—10. But the disciplined life he leads, Paul believes, should set an example for everyone in the church who is committed to serious discipleship.

The contest (*agōn*) motif is found elsewhere in Paul's letters. Phil. 3:14 is an example. Not that it was part of his Jewish heritage, but the typically Greek preoccupation with the development of the body through competitive and noncompetitive sports was part of the way of life in every Greco-Roman town and city across the Empire, including Hellenized Palestine, as Josephus bears witness.

In the fashion of other NT writers, Paul calls attention to life as a race to run and a wreath to win (2 Tim. 4:7–8; on the wreath, see 1 Pet. 5:4, James 1:12, Rev. 2:10, and cf. Wisd. of Sol. 5:15f.). But Paul's image is not perfect, for only one contestant can be declared the winner, whereas in the Christian life Paul rightly wants all to be winners. The emphasis must fall on the admonition that follows, "Like them, run to win!" (v. 24b NEB). Then as now "run for your life" had both literal and spiritual significance.

Suddenly, Paul's metaphor is directly applied to the writer himself (vv. 26–27). He is a runner straining toward the goal, not unsure of his direction. He is a boxer who aims to land his blows, not fan the air with a wild flailing. He continues rigorous training to be at his best. "I pummel my body" need not be conceived as an ascetic subjection of his physical body, if it be remembered that *sōma* for Paul basically refers to the total self, his whole person, in orientation toward God. He disciplines himself in a life of discipleship.

Following through the metaphor, Paul concedes the possibility of his own failure in the contest. A trainer and herald (*keryx*) for others, he might lose out himself and miss the prize if he did not keep in constant training, follow the rules, and give of his best. There was no easy victory for them or for him: "Lest after preaching to others I myself should be disqualified" (v. 27b). Against the cockiness he sometimes exhibits, this recognition of his own condition needs to be taken seriously in drawing a portrait of Paul the veteran campaigner.

*Gospel: Mark 1:40–45.* The story of the cleansing of a leper is the third healing story recounted by Mark to illustrate the special power and authority of Jesus in combating the powers of evil that hold humanity in thrall. In preparation for a study of the episode it would be helpful to reread the Torah section on leprosy, its treatment, and the appropriate ritual forms for rehabilitation (Leviticus 13—14). A complicated ceremony involving a guilt offering as well as the conventional burnt and cereal offerings was required before the cured person could be pronounced ritually clean. With the commanding word of Jesus, "Be clean!" and the touch of his hand, cure is effected and the official niceties are recommended.

The story reads smoothly in the RSV translation; "being moved with pity" describes Jesus' attitude. Another manuscript reading, however, probably gives the older form; "being angry, he stretched out his hand . . . ." How are we to understand this early and difficult reading? It is expressive of the hostility Jesus felt toward the disease and toward every other force in human life that militates against God's plan for wholeness *(shalom)* and salvation. He knew that God willed life not death, health not illness, salvation not judgment. He was deeply conscious, here and always, of the Kingdom of God in struggle against every antagonist of the divine will.

Mark's language is vigorous and striking throughout. In v. 43 it is said that Jesus "sternly charged him and sent him away at once." Literally the Greek text can be rendered, "He roared at him and drove him out." Originally the language may have been expressive of the command that the illness must no longer prevail, as in the order "Be muzzled," that is, be quiet, spoken to the unclean spirit tyrannizing the man in the synagogue (1:25). Mark believes that the time for the full disclosure of who Jesus is has not yet come; he must remain incognito. Nevertheless, despite necessity for this secrecy, God cannot be hidden. The truth will out (v. 45). Still, there is no indication that those who have experienced this healing power of God in action are brought to full faith. They are in the earliest stages of a belief which, for Mark, cannot be consummated short of the cross.

The tradition remembers that Jesus does not stand outside the Torah. He recognizes and advises the proper procedure for priestly approval in order that the healed man may be rehabilitated into society (v. 44). His quarrel was not with the Torah so much as with the scribes' and Pharisees' attitude toward and use of the Torah.

## HOMILETICAL INTERPRETATION

Since the readings from the OT and the Gospel both deal with healing lepers, the preacher may choose to weave the sermon from these two threads and leave the Second Lesson uninvolved. There would certainly be nothing amiss in such a procedure, especially since 1 Cor. 9:24–27 lies at such a great distance from healing stories. The fact is, Paul is hardly the one to approach for either discussion or cases of healing. In Acts, Luke portrays the ministry of Paul as attendant with miracles of blessing and cursing, but Paul himself is noticeably quiet on the subject. What that means is not clear. Most likely two factors are at work. First, that Paul's opponents—those whom he calls super-apostles—flashed miracles generously as proof of their ordination; maybe Paul overreacts. Second, Paul's definition of ministry was shaped by the cross—his life style was cruciform; crosses and miracles do not fit easily into the same frame.

So, let the preacher proceed one Sunday without Paul. The two healings offer more than can be handled in one message anyway. For example, both healings witness to God's merciful reach beyond the barriers respected by most religion: Elisha reached beyond the Jews to a Syrian; Jesus reached beyond the community to one who was isolated and pronounced socially and religiously unclean. After two thousand years, such a message still sounds strange and unacceptable to many church ears. Of course, there is applause for those who long ago and far away ministered according to the impartial grace of God, but "today our situation is different." Or again, a little-heard message lies in the loud, screaming, yelling hassle involved in both healings. The proud spirit of Naaman fussed and argued and protested Elisha's instructions for healing. And as our exegete has made vividly clear, Jesus' act of cleansing the leper was a battle with forces of evil. Read the text carefully. As in other Marcan miracle stories, the battle is joined between God and Satan. Evil does not roll over and play dead; there is shouting and anger and violence in a healing act. Somewhere, somehow the church concluded Jesus was pensive and recessive, soft of voice and gentle of touch; his words caressed the mind like warm oil and his healing hand was as soft as a baby's breath. Maybe, but at least listen to Mark. Jesus was not pitted against leprosy but against the power that destroys human life and dignity. Little has changed: improving the human lot of one person is still a big hassle; one can still grow quite weary in well-doing, especially when close friends and relatives who appear much more religious than you do seem not to be exercised at all about the matter.

If the preacher decides to focus upon the two healings, two cautions may be appropriate. First, beware of overdoing the symbolism—leprosy is sin, the Jordan is baptism, and so forth; once a preacher sets out on the symbolism journey, listeners grow suspicious that everything means something, and therefore nothing means anything. Second, beware of the old contrasts between Christianity and Judaism based on the images of Jesus touching to heal while Elisha sent instructions through a messenger. Such sermons are often arrogant, putting black hats on Jews and white hats on Christians.

Preachers who are stubborn and insist that there must be a discoverable reason why all *three* of the lections were chosen for today are the ones who regularly wrestle with *all* the texts, holding on with both hands and saying, "I will not let you go until you bless me." Very likely these preachers discerned before reading these comments that there lies at the heart of all three texts one fundamental principle: obedience. To be sure, obedience is variously conceived in the three passages, each carrying a different theological perspective, but it is unmistakably common to all.

In the Elisha-Naaman story, obedience is the path to healing. It is that simple. To obey is to hear and to do. To obey is better than sacrifice; to hearken, than the fat of rams. Do this and you will be well. The problems with obedience in this story are both practical and theological. The human spirit resists being told what to do and offers as more pleasing alternatives a variety of gifts and acts appropriate to one's pride. The theological problem lies in a widely felt resistance to any favor of God's being made contingent or conditional. Washing in the Jordan is distasteful enough; doing it as the necessary condition of healing is even more distasteful for those who insist absolutely that God's grace is always and everywhere free and without condition. However strongly one has embraced the view of grace as unconditional, it might be helpful to ponder whether some have reversed the conditions so that rather than saying obedience is a condition of grace, they have insisted that grace be a condition of obedience. Who is putting conditions on whom?

In 1 Cor. 9:24–27, obedience is operative as regular discipline so that body, mind, and spirit are kept in subjection to the will of God. Like an athlete undisciplined and untrained, the Christian who indulges all the faculties as proof of freedom in Christ will not finish the race or gain the prize. The analogy is too rigorous for some tastes, smacking of legalism and a merit system. Certainly Paul's analogy does raise those ancient ghosts. For others, the paragraph recalls old entanglements with individualistic pietism of a self-serving kind. That too is understandable. But it might help to allay these fears if it is remembered that Paul applies this discipline to himself, one who had already tossed out works-righteousness as garbage and who did not assume that having preached to others carried enough merit to gain him a passing grade. It is easier to be a preacher than a Christian. The image of the Christian as a disciplined person may be worth a second look.

Mark's story of Jesus healing a leper presents obedience not as a condi-

tion of being healed but as a response to being healed. "Go, show yourself
to the priest and offer for your cleansing what Moses commanded" is not in
pursuit of God's favor but in gratitude for it. The call for an act of obedience
*after* rather than *before* healing is in harmony with the basic perspective of
Scripture. The commandments at Sinai *followed* deliverance at the Red
Sea; instructions in Christian living *follow* the proclamation of God's
gracious initiative in Jesus Christ. It is both erroneous and regrettable that
some preachers—in fact, some churches—reverse the sequence and make
all faith responses preconditions of God's grace. Apparently out of fear that
grace and gratitude will not or cannot accomplish all the oughts and
shoulds, pressure is applied first to the believer and then to God. Pressure
on the believer lies in the insistence that full obedience is necessary in order
to receive God's favor; pressure on God lies in the proud recital of obedient
acts. The final product hardly resembles the quality of life created by the
preaching and hearing of the gospel.

None of these comments is intended to discard obedience as a Christian
trait—by no means! What does need to be remembered, however, is that
healing or forgiveness or grace or love are not strategies of God to force
changes in us, either by being withheld or by being given on condition. If in
doubt, just ask any father who has made the dreadful error of saying to a
child, "If you make good grades, Daddy will love you," or, no less
damaging, "Since Daddy loves you, you must make good grades." Grades
may improve a bit, but who cares? Something of far greater value has been
severely wounded, even killed.

## The Seventh Sunday after the Epiphany

| Lutheran | Roman Catholic | Episcopal | Pres/UCC/Chr | Meth/COCU |
|---|---|---|---|---|
| Isa. 43:18–25 | Isa. 43:18–19, 21–22, 24b–25 | Isa. 43:18–25 | Isa. 43:18–25 | Isa. 43:15–25 |
| 2 Cor. 1:18–22 | 2 Cor. 1:18–22 | 2 Cor. 1:18–22 | 2 Cor. 1:18–22 | 2 Cor. 1:18–22 |
| Mark 2:1–12 | Mark 2:1–12 | Mark 2:1–12 | Mark 2:1–12 | Mark 2:1–12 |

### EXEGESIS

*First Lesson: Isa. 43:15–25.* This Sunday's reading is a portion of a
larger section, 43:14—44:5, in which the Exilic Singer of Salvation declares
God's purpose to liberate his stricken people from bondage. This restored

people will be a sign to and a means of conversion for the Gentiles (43:10; 44:8; 55:4-5).

With Westermann, one might identify three clusters in this portion of the chapter, vv. 8-15, 16-21, and 22-28. V. 14 unmistakably refers to the conquest of the Babylonians by the Persian king, Cyrus the Great, in 538 B.C., a momentous event which this prophet interprets theologically as Yahweh's use of a heathen king to be his messiah (*mashiach*) or anointed in an event of salvation for Israel (45:1; cf. 44:28). This oracle may have ended with v. 15 in which Yahweh is praised as the Holy One, the Creator of Israel, and the King of Israel.

God's involvement in the history of Israel as Saviour was initially and decisively shown in the event of the exodus from Egypt. There Israel became God's people. In vv. 16-17 the prophet-poet describes the escape through the Red Sea and the destruction of the Egyptian army as the waters closed over them (cf. also 41:17-20; 42:16). The prophet then calls for a recognition of the present as the scene of a new act of salvation: "Remember not the former things, nor consider the things of old. Behold, I am doing a new thing" (vv. 18-19a).

It is a new time of exodus, a summons to passage into a new world of Yahweh's making! A way in the wilderness, water in the wilderness, rivers in the desert, safety from wild animals—all this God offers and Israel will live to praise him for it. The mention of the animals honoring Yahweh reminds us that this prophet in a special way has a theology of nature that brings together creation and redemption.

The concluding vv. 22-25 actually form part of a trial speech which becomes explicit in v. 26. The text probably is a critique of Israel's sacrificial worship, putting Second Isaiah in company with other prophets like Amos, Hosea, Isaiah, Micah, and Jeremiah. Westermann translates v. 24:

> Not for me did you buy sweet cane with your money,
> not me did you satisfy with the fat of your sacrifices.
> You made me serve—with your sins;
> wearied me with your iniquities.

The devastating charge here is that they have denied God his rightful lordship by making him into a *servant*. Now we can understand the difficult statement of v. 23 to mean that God never really demanded their sacrifices and their incense at all. That was *their doing*, not his. They made him suit their fancies!

Despite all this sorry history the extravagant mercy of God is such that he refuses to hold their sins to account (v. 25). Forgiveness is granted. A new start is given. The future holds promise.

*Second Lesson: 2 Cor. 1:18–22.* It is generally concluded that this lesson is part of an overture, ironic in tone, to the reestablishment of mutual confidence between Paul and the Corinthian church after the relationship between them had been under a severe strain. The letter was probably written from Macedonia, perhaps in Philippi, where Paul, deeply disturbed and anxious about the situation, intercepted Titus and heard the welcome news of the Corinthians' eagerness for reconciliation.

Some misunderstandings remained. The Corinthians were miffed because Paul's proposed double visit—first on his way to Macedonia and then again on his return—had been cancelled (vv. 15–16). Evidently this abrupt change in plans gave occasion for his critics to complain that he was just the type of unstable person who was capable of saying "Yes" and "No" in the same breath (v. 17). This "Yes" and "No" brings to mind a saying of Jesus' (Matt. 5:37), and Paul may have been alluding to a sayings-tradition which was later incorporated into the written gospel (cf. James 5:12).

Paul rejects any allegation of instability or capriciousness, insisting that though his travel plans had to be changed (v. 23; 2:1) he has always remained unswerving in his preaching of the gospel. It has never been for him a "Yes" ("I think so and so") followed immediately by a "No" ("But on the other hand . . . "). The intensity of his repudiation of the charge is indicated by the confirmatory oath, "As surely as God is faithful." This has always been the nature of his preaching and his mission planning (v. 18a). The very heart of the gospel is affirmation, not denial. It is the "Yes" of salvation—God's acceptance of sinful humanity in Jesus Christ, not the "No" of judgment and rejection. The implication is that the nature of the preaching must determine the nature of the preacher. The preacher's words and work must match the word and the work of the gospel.

The "promises of God" in v. 20 are the messianic salvation passages in the Scriptures, referred to also in Rom. 9:4; 15:8; Gal. 3:14, and frequently in the NT. To the early church, as to Paul, these divine promises had found their fulfillment in the person of Jesus the Messiah. Christ is the supreme Yes-sayer; Paul can be no less.

That assurance, the apostle maintains, is why the congregation at worship can say "Amen!" The response came from the temple and synagogue services (Deut. 27:15f.; Neh. 5:13; 8:6; Ps. 41:14) into Jewish and gentile Christian worship (cf. 1 Cor. 14:16), one of a few Semetic expressions borrowed for a Greek Christian vocabulary. By their "Amen!" the Corinthians had participated in Paul's preaching of the gospel in their midst.

Paul asserts that he and they are secured in Christ by God himself, who consecrated Paul and his associates for the mission work they carry on (v. 21). It is God who has certified them (v. 22). It is he who has empowered them by his Spirit, which is an initial installment (*arrabōn*) of what is yet to be theirs (cf. 2 Cor. 5:5). "Seal" (v. 22) is used in the OT both literally and figuratively to refer to a security, or as a substitute for a signature. Very early in Christian language it came to refer to baptism, perhaps influenced by its use in initiation rites in mystery cults. Serving in the name of such a God, for Paul, can only mean integrity of purpose and uncompromising commitment to the truth of the gospel.

*Gospel: Mark 2:1–12.* The healing of a paralytic in Mark heads a pre-Marcan collection of five stories in which Jesus is at loggerheads with the rabbis about his message and activity (2:1—3:6). The story before us is actually a composite, consisting of a healing story framing a theological dispute about forgiveness of sin. In the judgment of many scholars, the two were originally dissociated, vv. 1–5a and 11–12 constituting the healing story, and vv. 5b–10 the conflict between Jesus and the teachers of Law over the forgiveness of sin. The early church certainly believed it had the delegated authority to forgive sins in the name of Jesus and based that prerogative on the authority of Jesus (see Matt. 9:8; 18:18; John 20:23). It was a deep insight that correlated these two stories, for it is certain that Jesus himself understood his healing ministry as going beyond the effecting of cures (Matt. 12:28 = Luke 11:20).

Nothing is said about when this incident occurred, only that Jesus was "at home" in Capernaum (v. 1). He is sought out by so many people that the little house is crowded. Many stood outside, getting as close to the door as they could in order to listen. The ordinary one-room house of a Palestinian peasant was roofed with branches and mud overlaying wooden cross beams. Stairs leading to the roof would not normally be a feature of such a house, but would be reserved for those of more well-to-do citizens.

Nothing is said about the faith of the paralytic in seeking out the Galilean healer, only about the faith of the friends who carry him. Perhaps this detail is intended to highlight the fact that the healings for Mark are not conditioned by the sufferer's attitude but are wholly the miraculous work of God. In the continuation of the story at v. 11, Jesus addresses the sick man: "Rise, take up your pallet and go home." The crowd is amazed and glorifies God, recognizing that this was no ordinary healing: "We never saw anything like this!"

Mark's story of the conflict with the Torah teachers over forgiveness opens up the deeper dimensions of Jesus' healing work. In postbiblical Judaism sickness is regarded as a punishment for sin. The Babylonian Talmud reports a saying, "The sick man will not get up from his sickness until all his sins have been forgiven" (b. Ned. 41a). Jesus says, "My son, your sins are forgiven" (v. 5). Elsewhere he questions the popular explanation of affliction (Luke 13:1–5; John 9:2).

The reaction provoked suggests that this was more than a prophetic assurance that God has forgiven this man (vv. 6–7). Through Jesus, it is assumed, God was actually at work forgiving and healing. Something of this implicit claim to divine authority is sensed by his critics, who correctly insist that only God can forgive sins (v. 7). Indeed, the rabbis taught that not even the Messiah would have that authority. Nor does Jesus deny their claim. But, he implies, delegated authority has been given to him to forgive sin. Within the words we may hear the challenge to the ministry of forgiveness practiced by the early church and also the defense of that ministry.

The episode discloses Jesus' constant concern with the theological issues implicit in sickness and health as forms of forgiveness and salvation (wholeness). In this sense, as the Gospel writers know, the healing ministry, no less than the preached word, is a demonstration of the presence and power of the kingdom in action.

### HOMILETICAL INTERPRETATION

Preachers who seek to sustain the meaning of Epiphany throughout this season can on this Sunday move in one of two directions. They can speak either of the new thing God is doing, or of the agency by which he does it.

By the first approach Epiphany is God's revealing himself in doing a new thing, creating a new experience. In Isa. 43:15–25, the new event is a new exodus from the Exile to Israel's homeland. It is no less an act of God, no less meaningful for Israel and for the world, no less dramatic in its process, no less stirring for its beneficiaries, no less demanding upon its participants, than the first exodus from Egypt. The simple fact that the return of the exiles is portrayed in the language and imagery of the Exodus places it as a central and formative event in the life and mission of Israel.

That which is new in 2 Cor. 1:18–22 is the relationship between Paul and the church in Corinth. The exegete has noted something of the stormy relationship between Paul and this church. If one reads 2 Corinthians 10—13 before the chapter containing our lection for today, one can not only understand but experience Paul's lines about affliction and comfort and his reasons for not returning to Corinth for what would have been a painful visit. If 2 Corinthians 10—13 is the painful letter to which Paul refers (2 Cor. 2:1–4), then it is clear with what joy and relief Paul could now write in a spirit of forgiveness and reconciliation. To have been separated from this church geographically had been anguish enough; to have been engaged in charges, countercharges, criticism, and personal attack was surely heartbreaking. But let bygones be bygones, says Paul; forgiveness and reconciliation must rule our hearts and launch a new day for the church and for Paul's relation to it. The Corinthians are still miffed that Paul changed his plans about visiting them but the general mood of the apostle is to clarify, forgive, accept, and initiate a new climate in the church. That there can be such a new day is beyond any doubt; this is what God is doing in Christ Jesus, the guarantee of which is the presence of God's Spirit among and within them.

Mark 2:1–12 carries a story of God's new work in Jesus' pronouncement of forgiveness of sin. In a sense, forgiveness is the epitome of the human experience of God doing a new thing. The word itself is the title for some of the most powerful and moving stories of the Bible, for example, that of Joseph receiving the brothers who had sold him into slavery. The word signifies one of the most complex moments in all human relationships: the giving and receiving of forgiveness. The word is essential in any discussion of the meaning of the cross. Perhaps no word has gathered to itself so many beautiful images of the new: Forgiveness is dawn, birth, snowfall, resurrection, springtime, a new year, release, jubilee, pardon, a new creation, and countless other analogies. But in all this beauty and promise, the experience itself remains surprisingly rare. Why? Is it because it seems too good to be true? Is it because forgiving seems too easy, too permissive, too condoning? Or is it rather because forgiveness is meaningless in a society that sees nothing to forgive or to be forgiven? Any treatment at all of Mark 2:1–12 will demand careful and sensitive reflection upon Jesus' words, "My son, your sins are forgiven."

If the theme of "the new" is developed on the basis of one or all of the texts for today, the preacher will probably want to anticipate and deal with two questions that linger disturbingly in many minds. One relates to the matter of identifying with some assurance that new thing which God is doing. It is not difficult to reflect on the past, especially as it is narrated by believers, and concur in the witness that God was at work here or there, leading, renewing, reconciling, and healing. But how does a believer look upon the present scene—political, social, and personal—and say with any kind of confidence, "God is here doing a new thing"? What criteria are there for making such judgments? The prophet interpreted the rise of Persia and King Cyrus as God's occasion for a new exodus. Does today's preacher make similar interpretations about currents in our world? Or, in terms of smaller groups and individuals, can reconciliation and forgiveness be named and celebrated as acts of God among us? If not, why not? Faith in the past tense is safe; in the present tense, risky. Some who want the preacher to stick with the Bible may actually be insisting that sermons deal with the past.

A second question that impinges on these and countless other texts may be stated in this way: If God is doing a *new* thing, how are we to regard the past? Some churches are caught in strong crosscurrents. On the one hand, the church is trying to be nourished by her memory, to claim her roots, to build again a reservoir of Scripture and tradition to overcome the privatism that has so weakened the body. With new intensity, the believing community is trying to say again, "Abraham is our father" and to reject the tendency of our recent past to draw the parenthesis of interest tightly around the "Now" generation. On the other hand, the church is experiencing the "born-again" phenomenon within the membership. Some are claiming a new experience of God so radical as to be discontinuous with the past, even if that past was spent in the church-school and worship. It is not uncommon to hear testimonies that highlight the new by being severely critical of previous home and church experience. Does that new thing which God is doing stand in such sharp discontinuity with the past? What is to be done with yesterday? Isaiah described God's new act as an exodus. The description suggests that Israel's past interpreted the present; Israel's present continued the past. Memory and hope inform each other.

A second approach by which Epiphany may be nourished and quickened through today's lections involves giving primary attention not to the new thing God is doing but to the agency by which God is doing it. Let the mind wander over the texts with this in view: King Cyrus of Persia, Saul of Tarsus, Jesus of Nazareth. Does any nerve twitch? Cyrus, a Persian king, is God's shepherd, God's anointed (Christ), to lead a new exodus? But he is a foreigner! He is not one of us! The first exodus was led by one of *ours* (we forgave his Egyptian beginnings). Is there no good candidate for the post among *us*? The prophet had a vision of God who is Lord of the Nations, who thinks of Israel, yes, but who thinks also of the world. The prophet understood that God accomplishes his purposes through persons who may not worship him, through events that may seem totally secular. Could Isaiah's audience, can we, wrap our hearts and minds around such a grand vision and say, "Amen"? If so, it will affect not only how we read the Bible but also how we read the newspaper.

Or think about Paul as God's agent of reconciliation in Corinth. This Paul is the same man who persecuted the church of God and tried to destroy it. This is the Paul who claimed to be an apostle "untimely born," insisting that he saw the risen Lord near Damascus in Syria. This is the missionary who was always in trouble with friends and foes: doubted, ostracized, chased, beaten, imprisoned. This is the minister who founded the Corinthian church and who promised to make two return visits but changed his mind. He says "Yes" and then says "No"; yes and no can hardly effect reconciliation. And yet here he is, pastoring and forgiving in love, rejoicing over the progress of God's healing word in that community. You never know, do you?

Or consider Jesus of Nazareth, speaking God's forgiving word which initiates a new day in a person's life. In this text, the preacher will want to be instructed by the exegete in order not to get sidetracked by the healing story which surrounds the pronouncement of forgiveness. It is characteristic of Mark to wrap one story around another, as he does with the exorcism in Capernaum (1:21–28), the healing of the woman with a flow of blood (5:21–43), the cleansing of the temple (11:12–26), and others. Unquestionably, the issue of forgiving sins dominates this text. The critics of Jesus have properly sensed what is at stake here: Can Jesus of Nazareth say, "Your sins are forgiven"? Is not this Joseph's son? Are not his sisters and brothers known to us? The critics take offense at him, for only God can forgive sin, just as the synagogue took offense at the church which pronounced the forgiveness of sin. Can the church say, "Your sins are forgiven"?

The church, in the exercise of piety, has often developed rituals of self-disqualification. These little ceremonies usually begin with the question, "Who am I that I should presume to act or speak for God?" God is doing a new thing, but with and through whom? No one seems to be qualified. This one has a sordid past, that one lacks the proper education, and another confesses some doubts. Had the early church thought in these terms, you and I would never have heard the gospel. After all, look over the membership of those assemblies. Do you see anyone who is qualified?

But God does not delay his new work waiting for volunteers; he makes assignments. God continues to find a Cyrus here, a Paul there—and of course Jesus of Nazareth is still with us.

# The Eighth Sunday after the Epiphany

| Lutheran | Roman Catholic | Episcopal | Pres/UCC/Chr | Meth/COCU |
|----------|----------------|-----------|--------------|-----------|
| Hos. 2:14–16, (17–18) 19–20 | Hos. 2:14b, 15b, 19–20 | Hos. 2:14–23 | Hos. 2:14–20 | Hos. 2:14–23 |
| 2 Cor. 3:1b–6 | 2 Cor. 3:1–6 | 2 Cor. 3:(4–11) 17—4:2 | 2 Cor. 3:17—4:2 | 2 Cor. 3:1b–6 |
| Mark 2:18–22 | Mark 2:18–22 | Mark 2:18–22 | Mark 2:18–22 | Mark 2:18–22 |

## EXEGESIS

*First Lesson: Hos. 2:14–23.* Hosea was active in the last years of the Northern Kingdom, prophesying during and following the reign of Jereboam II (784–744 B.C.). Deep feelings saturate his words: anguish over the infidelity of his people, alarm at the impending doom that will befall the nation, reassurance in the hope of an ultimate salvation. He is the first to speak of a promised new convenant between God and his people, the fulfillment of the Exodus event—a theme whose trajectory can be traced through Jeremiah, Ezekiel, Qumran, and which culminates in Jesus.

The background for what Hosea has to say to his people in God's name, and the reason for the language of sacred marriage between Yahweh and Israel, is to be found in the popularity of Canaanite cult practices and holy marriage (sacred prostitution) among the Israelites of his day. Hosea decries the claim that the Canaanite Baal is the true source of Israel's agricultural prosperity (2:5), insisting that the God of their nomadic fathers is the Giver of crops and flocks (2:8). In a stinging indictment, he blames the priests for the people's defection; they are accused of lacking the necessary knowledge of God, by which Hosea means not conceptual, theological understanding, but a wholehearted dependence upon and devotion to Yahweh.

Our lesson forms part of Hosea's description of how Israel will be reeducated and renewed after the chastisement of judgment has come upon it. Chap. 2, especially vv. 9–13, has pictured a torrent of calamities poured upon Israel for her religious adultery. With the beginning of our lection, there is a surprising change of tone, as if the prophet cannot bear to speak another word of death and desolation. In v. 14 we have a picture of Yahweh wooing his unfaithful wife, "I will allure her," leading her back into the wilderness where, in the Exodus, their life together had begun (cf. 11:8).

The tradition of the wilderness in Israel's experience came to bear double meanings. For many, like Ezekiel, it was remembered as a place of confusion, rebellion, and God's heavy hand in the national history (for example, Ezekiel 20). For Hosea and Jeremiah (2:1–3) it was seen as a symbol of a pristine loyalty to their God, a blessed time of trustful dependence upon his leadership, a sign of his redemption for his people. Israel will once again respond to Yahweh as it did in the time of the first trek out of Egypt (v. 15b; cf. 11:1). A whole new beginning will be made. Yahweh alone will be named Israel's husband.

In 2:16–23 the prophet describes the content of that wilderness experience as the formulation of a new covenant. In an extraordinary way Hosea visualizes the covenant affecting even the natural order, the world of nature and its animal life. Israel's rift with Yahweh has disturbed its basic relationship with subhuman creatures. Enmity and fear prevail between people and animals. But a disordered creation will be restored to harmony (v. 18; cf. Isa. 11:6–9); warfare will be brought to an end (v. 18; cf. Isa. 2:2–4; Mic. 4:3–4). The inclusive covenant which embraces persons and all living creatures is a very old concept of God's relationship to his world (Gen. 9:8–17). The new covenantal relationship involves persons in peaceful relationship to the animal and human environments. Then at last God can say, "You are my people" and they can reply, "You are our God" (v. 23).

*Second Lesson: 2 Cor. 3:1–6.* From Hosea's prediction of a covenant that will be made in the new day of salvation, the lessons move to the famous passage in which the Christian Jew, Paul of Tarsus, deliberates on the establishment of a ministry of the new covenant. Sorting out the correspondence that passed between Paul and the Corinthian church, we may assign this portion to a lengthy segment of a letter that followed the writing of 1 Corinthians 2:14—7:4 (1 Cor. 6:14—7:1 is generally recognized to be a separate exhortation). The theme of this letter-fragment is a sustained defense of Paul's apostolic credentials, presumably in response to opponents who denied them.

Paul is sensitive to the charges of self-appointment and inflated self-esteem brought against him by his critics (v. 1; cf. 4:5, 5:12, 6:4). The language he has just used—"Christ always leads us in triumph" (2:14); "We are the aroma of Christ" (2:15); the implication: *We* are sufficient for these things (2:16); "We are commissioned by God" (2:17)—made him vulnerable to the accusation. He must explain himself. The confirmation of his own God-given apostolate, he reiterates, is demonstrated in the very existence of the church of Christ in Corinth. They themselves constitute a living document of recommendation of his commission and his preaching.

The Greek text in v. 2 is read by the RSV as a letter, written on *your* hearts, to be read by all. In this case, the dependent clause would refer to their deep affection for him as their father in the faith. The best manuscript evidence, however, would lead us to prefer the marginal reading of RSV: written on *our* hearts, expressive of Paul's deep affection for these Corinthian friends. They are a letter from Christ to the world, written not with pen and ink but with the Spirit of God, and delivered by Christ's messenger, Paul.

This alone is the ground of Paul's confidence in himself and in his work: what has happened and is happening to them. The sufficiency, however, is not his but God's, on whom he relies and who empowers him to service. This recognition of his unconditional dependency from first to last upon the God he serves is crucial to a proper understanding of the apostle Paul.

Paul has a way of letting one image suggest another, one word-sound evoke another, in something of the fashion of word association that characterized rabbinic exegesis. The stone/heart metaphor brings him again to the gospel as he understands it. It is the new and perfect covenant between God and his people, foreshadowed by the first covenant of the Torah. We have heard Hosea's anticipation of an eschatological covenant (Hos. 2:18); we recall Jeremiah's and Ezekiel's development of this great hope. Paul associates the concept directly with Jesus (1 Cor. 11:25); he refers to it nine times in his letters. It is mentioned seventeen times in Hebrews and cited in toto thirty-three times in the NT. The word "covenant" in the first and primary instance refers to the new relationship with God through Christ, proclaimed as good news. Paul juxtaposes Torah covenant (*gramma*, or document) with Spirit covenant (*pneuma*) as a death and life issue (3:6; cf. the same contrast in Rom. 2:29; 7:6), and triumphantly asserts that God has made him and his colleagues ministers of this new covenant.

Notice the progression: Who is sufficient? (2:16): We are sufficient! (by implication, 2:16). Our sufficiency is from God (3:5). God has made us sufficient as ministers (3:6).

*Gospel: Mark 2:18–22.* The Gospel lesson today presents us with several sayings of Jesus, together with some extensions that we may best understand as interpretations originating in the early church. In the string of unrelated episodes that comprises this section of Mark's Gospel (2:1—3:6), we come upon an incident centering on the issue of fasting as a religious discipline (2:18–20). To this material, Mark or his source has appended a saying of Jesus' consisting of several proverbs which most likely were used on another occasion, since they are unrelated to the wedding imagery of vv. 18–20.

Mark provides a setting that is not followed, in this instance, by the other synoptists. Noticing the practices of the disciples of John the Baptist and the Pharisees in special acts of fasting, some people raise a questions about the absence of fasting among Jesus' disciples (v. 18). That this religious discipline is also of special concern to the early church may be seen in the way Mark makes it a defense of the disciples' conduct, not Jesus'; that is, the church is defending its own practices of fasting (Acts 13:2f.; 14:23; 1 Cor. 9:24–27). That defense is to be found in the rhetorical question of v. 19, as many scholars agree: "Do the wedding guests (literally sons of the bridechamber) fast while the bridegroom is with them (that is, during the wedding)?" Jesus' response, "Do wedding guests fast?" is to say: This is the day of salvation! It calls for rejoicing, not mourning! This attitude does not mean the abrogation of all special religious acts, but it does make devotional practices instrumental to faith-convictions.

Elaborating this saying, the early church used it to justify the reintroduction of fasting into congregational life. With vv. 19b–20 they extended the saying into an allegory of the Passion, when the Messiah-bridegroom would be put to death and fasting would be appropriate until his return.

The appended sayings in vv. 21–22 may be secular proverbs employed by Jesus to state dramatically the radical novelty of his message of the kingdom and its salvation. Clothing and wine, like the wedding feast, were familiar symbols in rabbinic teaching for the new age of God's favor. (Cf. Ps. 102:26.) New cloth is not suitable to patch an old garment. New wine is not for old wineskins. This is a familiar refrain in the message of Jesus. The new thing is really, truly new, not a patched up version of the old. It cannot be accomodated to old structures, old formulas, old practices. It is the new time of salvation!

HOMILETICAL INTERPRETATION

Epiphany, the manifestation of Jesus Christ to the world, brings into sharp focus a whole set of questions, the pursuit of which is the task of the whole believing community and of each member personally. All these questions revolve around the patterns of continuity and discontinuity which are appropriate for living the gospel in the world.

For example, when one thinks of the relation of church and world, continuity must be affirmed, for God is creator of all life and all life is the object of his seeking love. However, the church has been called out from the world to be God's agent for the ultimate redemption of the world. Discontinuity lies in the very nature of the case. When one thinks of Jesus Christ, continuity in terms of promise and fulfillment are basic to understanding the event. "In many and various ways God spoke of old to our fathers by the prophets; but in these last days he has spoken to us by a Son" (Heb. 1:1–2). However, the Christian faith sees in Jesus Christ a revelation of God unique among all revelations. There is a difference; there is discontinuity. When one thinks of the relation of the Christian faith to its parent Judaism, the memory of long and heated debates still unsettles the church. Matthew struggled with it: "I have not come to destroy the law and the prophets": "You have heard it said . . . but I say." Luke settled upon more continuity than discontinuity and wrote his two-volume work as a running narrative of Israel, Jesus, and the church. The Epistle to the Hebrews sought a philosophical resolution in a pattern of shadow (Judaism) and substance (Christianity). Paul affirmed the Law as holy, just, good, and of God, and yet he could testify to its power to lead one into zealous endeavors of self-righteousness. Shall we continue to worship in the synagogue? Yes, said some; No, said others. Shall we keep the Hebrew Scriptures as Scripture for the church? Of course, said some; Certainly not, said others. The final embrace of a Bible divided into OT and NT vividly perpetuates the church's struggle over these issues: one book, two parts.

Living in the twentieth century does not at all remove us from the discussion. Church and world are still in the conversation; Christians and Jews continue to talk along significant lines; and the followers of Jesus Christ now and then become serious about discussing these matters among themselves. When such conversations take place, the lections for today should be included.

Hos. 2:14–23 highlights continuity rather than discontinuity in the poetic descriptions of God's tenacious love that will not let his people go. The key word is covenant. To be sure, Israel has forgotten and broken the vows of that covenant, but alienation is not the final word. On the analogy of marriage and infidelity, and of reconciliation at God's—not Israel's—

initiative, Hosea beautifully though painfully portrays God's covenant love. Throughout Israel's faithlessness, God remains faithful. The faithfulness of God is the ground of all hope of salvation. It is God's faithfulness that renews the covenant, and the benefits of it reach beyond Israel to the nations, beyond the nations to all creation. Even animals and plants will know again the harmony of Eden. Paul picked up on this theme and exulted in the vision of all creation sharing in the redemption of God's children (Rom. 8:19–23). Slowly and painfully, we have now been forced to see that, if there is any redemption at all, plants and animals, earth and air, sky and sea will share in it.

Covenant is a word that conveys continuity. It gives meaning to a long story that is marred by doubt, disobedience, infidelity, pride and self-sufficiency. Our God is a covenant God who does not want a divorce. Covenant is probably the one word that makes the sixty-six books of the Bible one book.

Paul found the term and idea of covenant central to his view of God's relating to the world. In fact, Paul understands his vocation as that of a minister of the new covenant (2 Cor. 3:1–6). However, Paul found himself often stressing discontinuity; distinguishing between old and new covenants. Why did he, a Jew, place old and new in such sharp contrasts? Was it simply a typical case of the convert who paints the past in dark colors in order to affirm more vividly the present? That hardly accounts for it. Paul, who in calmer moments insisted that the roots are Abraham, Isaac, and Jacob, and that gentile Christians have been grafted in, was constantly questioned and contested about the validity of his ministry. Much of this opposition came from Christians who insisted upon continuity with Judaism, including the keeping of the Mosaic law. Although Paul could have claimed that continuity (Phil. 3:2ff.), he counted the legalism that had grown up around the law a violation of Christian freedom. Against these Judaizers Paul had to argue that his was the true gospel, his churches were genuinely churches, and his converts were truly Christians. These churches were, in fact, Paul's only public vindication of his ministry. You are my certification as a minister, he said to them.

Under conditions of debate, one thinks and writes not in continuities but discontinuities. The circumstance should flavor our interpretation of 2 Cor. 3:1–6, especially if we are inclined to fault Paul for fragmenting the faithfulness of God into old covenant and new covenant. There are differences between Moses and Christ, to be sure, but if Paul underscores those differences with expressions such as "written on the heart and not on stone" and "living Spirit and not dead letter," we need to recall the conflicts which engaged him. And unless we are engaged in similar conflicts, our continuing to stress new versus old hardly seems appropriate. Notes left on the podium after a debate is over hardly constitute a ready-made sermon outline for succeeding generations of speakers who do not recall the issue.

Mark 2:18–22 offers an interesting mixture of continuity and discontinuity. Mark includes the question about fasting in his section on conflicts between Jesus or his disciples (or both together) and Jewish authorities (2:1—3:6). As the exegete has made clear, this is plainly a story about fasting among Jesus' disciples; that is, the practice of fasting in the church. The dominant impression given by this pericope is that the rites and practices of the Christian community are discontinuous with the past in Judaism. One does not put a new patch on an old garment; neither does one put new wine in old skins. However, fasting, a ritual of Judaism, is conceived in the church as a way of observing the time of Christ's passion. But according to Mark, this is not a case simply of continuing a Jewish practice. Fasting was inappropriate when Christ was present (during the wedding) but became appropriate upon his death (when the groom was taken away). In other words, the issue is not one of whether Christians do or do not continue an ancient practice. The real issue is rather, whether the rituals of the faith are appropriate expressions of that faith.

Perhaps this is the note on which to close. The main thing may be not at all a question of continuity and discontinuity. It is more important for the community of faith to reflect upon its acts as a worshiping and believing fellowship and to ask whether or not those acts convey meaning and adequately express life before God. This critical self-appraisal might serve to disarm those guardians of the past and those champions of the present who cross swords in every assembly, sometimes without having paused to ask of the act in question, "Is it meet and right so to do?"

# The Transfiguration of Our Lord
## The Last Sunday after the Epiphany

| Lutheran | Roman Catholic | Episcopal | Pres/UCC/Chr | Meth/COCU |
|---|---|---|---|---|
| 2 Kings 2:1–12a | Dan. 7:9–10, 13–14 | 1 Kings 19:9–18 | Dan. 7:13–14 | 2 Kings 2:1–12a |
| 2 Cor. 3:12—4:2 | 2 Pet. 1:16–19 | 2 Pet 1:16–19 (20–21) | Rev. 1:4–8 | 2 Cor. 3:12—4:2 |
| Mark 9:2–9 | Mark 9:2–10 | Mark 9:2–9 | John 18:33–37 | Mark 9:2–9 |

## EXEGESIS

*First Lesson: 2 Kings 2:1–12a.* The Elijah-Elisha stories out of a Northern Kingdom tradition are a curious complex of historical and legendary

materials. The story of the ascension of Elijah in the presence of his
devoted disciple and successor, Elisha, is a striking example.

With the other major victories won in the struggle of Yahwism with
Tyrian Baalism, Elijah is conscious that his time is drawing to a close. He
and Elisha are traveling from Gilgal to Bethel and then on to Jericho. At
each place, they are met by members of the prophets' guild who warn
Elisha that his master will soon be taken from him. Elisha insists on
remaining with Elijah to the very end, though the prophet urges him to
remain behind, no doubt as a way of testing him, for he "knows" that it is
Elisha who will be appointed to carry on his work. At the Jordan, outside
Jericho, Elijah parts the waters as the two men walk dry-shod to the eastern
side. "What shall I do for you?" Elijah asks and Elisha responds, "Give me
a double share of your spirit" (2:9). Elisha is told that if he is witness to
Elijah's passing, then he will be qualified. He sees his master carried up in
the heavenly chariot. Elisha assumes the mantle of his teacher; he is
"clothed" with his power, and the sons of the prophets acknowledge him
as their leader (2:15).

Only two men in the OT are said to be worthy of passing from mortal life
directly into the presence of God: Enoch (Gen. 5:24) and Elijah. They alone
do not suffer the common human fate of death and descent to Sheol. Wind
and fire, here and elsewhere in the Bible, are symbols of the divine power in
judgment. Now at Elijah's final moments the fire and wind of God strike, in
the form of a chariot (*merkabah*) and horses (cf. Ezek. 1:4–28a; Isa. 66:15).
Elijah is swept up in Elisha's presence and disappears from sight. The
astonished disciple cries "My father, my father! The chariots of Israel and
its horsemen!" The cry is a lament for his lost leader, "my father, my
father," and perhaps a recognition of the divine power, greater than
all human strength, which Yahweh makes the strength of his people
(cf. 13:14).

The figure of Elijah became the center of an elaborate legend and messianic speculation in later Judaism. Mal. 4:5 testifies to a postexilic hope
that the prophet who was to come in the end time would be none other than
Elijah redivivus, a messenger of peace and redemption. In the early church
John the Baptist was regarded as the new Elijah (Mark 9:13 = Matt.
17:12–13; Matt. 11:14). Some thought that Jesus was Elijah redivivus (Mark
8:28, par.). We shall note in the Gospel lesson the rabbinic teaching that the
Messiah, when he came, would be attended by Moses and Elijah (Mark
9:4–5, par.).

*Second Lesson: 2 Cor. 3:12—4:2.* Today's lesson, like the Second
Lesson of the Eighth Sunday after the Epiphany, is drawn from a letter of
defense addressed by Paul to the Corinthians. The comparison Paul has

drawn between the written code of the Law and the life-giving Spirit has been elaborated in the intervening section (3:7–11) between the reading for last Sunday and that for today. It is the enduring splendor of the new against the transient glory of the old on which the apostle now reflects further. He develops a scriptural argument to support his case out of an obscure detail in the story of Moses and his people at Sinai which he reads in his own way (3:7, 11–12). The story should be read in full in Exod. 34:29–35. Paul does not claim that the Torah text was intended to mean what he finds in it. In the absence of any scriptural explanation of why Moses wore a veil, Paul interprets it to signify that Moses wishes to conceal from the people the fading of the divine glory from his face. By that means, Paul finds evidence that the covenant with Moses and his people was an interim arrangement (3:10–11; cf. Gal. 3:23–25). The details of Paul's exegesis may be questioned, but the theological insight that something new has happened is foundational to the way Jesus relates the good news of the imminent kingdom to the Law and the prophets (see, for example, Matt. 11:12–13 = Luke 16:16).

Then Paul reflects on the veil as a symbol of the dullness of mind of those under the old covenant (vv. 14–15) and, like the Isaiah oracle (25:7), he applies it also to the unbelieving Gentiles (4:3–4; cf. Rom. 1:22). What then, of the opposite condition? Christ, he maintains, can take away that dullness and blindness so that unveiled faces can permanently reflect his glory, just as the unveiled face of Moses temporarily reflected the glory of Yahweh (vv. 14, 16). It is this hope that enables Paul and his associates to preach the gospel openly and boldly (v. 12).

Vv. 17 and 18 are crucial to the argument. The Greek of v. 17 is simple and straightforward: "Now the Lord is the Spirit; where the Spirit of the Lord is, there is freedom." In the NT the Spirit is always understood christologically, as related to and consequent upon the Risen Lord. The Spirit is "the subjective complement of the objective fact of Christ." Thus Paul speaks of a turning to the Lord, who is none other than the Spirit, in whose presence there is freedom (v. 17) and life (v. 6c; cf. Rom 8:2). Because there is no clouding of our vision we can and do reflect unhindered the glory of Christ. All of us, not just the leaders, are now being transfigured into his likeness, from splendor to splendor (v. 18; cf. 1 Cor. 15:49).

Since this is the nature of our ministry (RSV, service; the word is *diakonia*) we cannot be downhearted (4:1). With a sly innuendo to the teachers opposing him in Corinth, Paul disavows any shameful deeds, acts of cunning, or distortion of the gospel. As he has insisted before, he and his colleagues use great boldness of speech (3:12), declaring the truth openly (is the opposition devious?). Preaching is the free statement of the unveiled truth!

*Gospel: Mark 9:2–9.* The visionary experience of the transfiguration of Jesus has been subject to widely divergent interpretations in scholarly circles. If we begin by asking what it meant for Mark, we may conclude that he understood it as a prophecy of the Resurrection, or the Parousia, or a confirmation of the messiahship of Jesus. With the church of his day, he is certain of the promised advent; in the reproof of Peter's enthusiasm (v. 6), however, there may be a reminder that the end is imminent but not immediate. Perhaps Mark was facing a church like that at Thessalonica, excited that the end was already beginning (2 Thess. 2:2).

The account of Moses as he began and again as he concluded the forty day period in the presence of Yahweh at Mount Sinai should be read again, in Exodus 29 and 34. Many of the details of the Gospel story are drawn from this ancient theophany. There is similarity, too, to Jewish views about the form of the end time. The appearance of Elijah and Moses with Jesus brings to mind the popular expectation of the Elijah prophet (Mal. 4:5) and the prophet like Moses (Deut. 18:15). The Gospel story intends to use the Exodus imagery typologically to declare that in Jesus salvation history is fulfilled, the new exodus has begun, led by God's Anointed One.

The glory of the Presence was reflected in the shining face of Moses (Exod. 34:29–30). God's Son was "transfigured"; he appeared in the dazzling garments of the heavenly world (Rev. 1:13; 4:4; 7:9). Paul believed that this ineffable radiance marked human life in Christ beginning with the present (Rom. 12:2; Phil. 3:21; and the Second Lesson for this Sunday). The "high mountain," "six days," and the "cloud" in vv. 2 and 7 are reminiscent of Exod. 24:16: "The glory of the Lord settled on Mount Sinai, and the cloud covered it six days; and on the seventh day he called to Moses out of the midst of the cloud." At the baptism of Jesus, the Voice from heaven had spoken to Jesus, "Thou art my beloved Son; with thee I am well pleased" (Mark 1:11). Here on the mountain, the Voice addresses the others, not Jesus, "This is my beloved Son; listen to him" (v. 7). In the context of Peter's refusal to listen to any talk of a suffering Messiah (8:31–32), the command "Listen to him" gains specific force. Peter must hear what he does not want to hear. The appearance of Elijah and Moses with the glorified Master would certainly be understood eschatologically by Jewish hearers.

Jesus marks the beginning of the new age of salvation, dawning in all its glory and promise. But the power at work in his miraculous healing and the glory disclosed in this visionary experience are anticipatory of what can become reality for his disciples only through the climactic events of his cross and resurrection. That explains the reference in v. 9 to another injunction to silence. Mark reserves full disclosure for the decisive events of cross and resurrection—for him the heart and center of the gospel message. Lent and Good Friday lie between the Last Sunday after the Epiphany and Easter Day.

## HOMILETICAL INTERPRETATION

The season of Epiphany concludes with the most dazzling array of texts, all of them openly and clearly participating in the primary sense of Epiphany: appearance of the Lord. Simply a first reading of these texts fills eye and ear with the glory of God. No one, of course, has ever seen God, but all the attending phenomena which both reveal and conceal are present: high mountains, lights, clouds, wind, chariots, the divine voice. One could almost do "sensory hermeneutics" here; that is, let the five senses apprehend the messages of the texts.

Very likely, the preacher will find this wealth of imagery a problem for the sermon. Texts that are especially rich in content or imagery bedazzle both speaker and hearer, and there is the temptation simply to repeat the words and describe the scenes as though this in itself constituted a message. Adjectives dance around and display themselves, but may not light anyone's path.

It would be wise, therefore, for purposes of the sermon, to focus upon one of the three texts. The natural choice would be to choose the transfiguration story in Mark 9:2–9 and let the other two nourish and enlighten. The exegesis has made the kinship among the passages quite clear. In concentrating upon Mark 9:2–9, one is interpreting not simply the story of Jesus' transfiguration but *Mark's* understanding and use of that story. Searching for Mark's message here will constrain and discipline our thinking even further, an important consideration when preaching from a text so full of the transcendent.

The transfiguration, drawing heavily upon Exodus 24—35 and 2 Kings 2 (cf. exegesis), is *the* epiphany in Mark. The account is similar to that of Jesus' baptism but differs in several key respects. The transfiguration occurs on a very high mountain, has its eschatological force heightened by the appearance of Moses and Elijah, and unlike the baptism is not a private experience of Jesus but a revelation to the disciples. The voice from heaven is addressed to them, not to Jesus. In fact, the disciples and their understanding or misunderstanding, so much a preoccupation of Mark, will probably serve as a key to the meaning of the text.

One means by which Mark conveys meaning is by the arrangement of his material. Where he places a story is revelatory of its meaning for him. The transfiguration story comes immediately after the confession of Peter at Caesarea Philippi. In that account Jesus rebukes Peter and commands silence following Peter's confession. Peter rebukes Jesus; Jesus rebukes

Peter. The scene carries the verbal violence of an exorcism and is wrapped not only in the pall of Jesus' approaching death but also in that of the disciples' complete lack of understanding. Death and cross-bearing hardly fit with any view of the Messiah which they had entertained. The pattern of their confusion and blindness, which runs through the entire Gospel, is perhaps most painfully visible here.

Perhaps we ought to pause here in our listening to Mark in order to become aware of where we stand while listening. The reader's point of identification with a text is a major factor in what is heard, and therefore in what is preached. In the text before us, do we identify with the disciples and see ourselves in a similar condition or do we identify with Jesus and stand in criticism of the twelve? The difference is not insignificant. Experience and observation argue for identification with the disciples.

Immediately after the shock, pain, and confusion of Caesarea Philippi, Mark places the transfiguration. Here the inner circle of disciples gets a glimpse of the eschaton and of the glory of Christ yet to be manifest; here they receive heaven's confirmation of who Jesus really is; here they are given a divine command to obey Jesus, even if his words are demanding or offensive or contrary to their expectations.

Mark's location of the story, therefore, argues for its function as encouragement to the disciples and hence to the church. A glimpse of the future is not too much to ask. At the high noon of tranquillity the church may sing, "I ask no dream, no prophet's ecstasy, no sudden rending of the veil of clay," but at the midnight of despair, it is not unreasonable to ask that one corner of the veil be lifted so that the shining glory be seen rather than the sweat and blood. Even being disciples on the bright side of Easter requires some nourishment other than the thin diet of fond memories of the Camelot of his earthly days. There must be hope. Without hope no one can live. And hope does not require much to stay alive. A cloud the size of a man's hand quickens hope of a drought broken. The doctor has only to say "I think we got it all" or "The pulse is stronger now" and hope goes leaping into tomorrow. So tenacious is hope's grasp on life that almost empty phrases such as "No news is good news" will keep one by the phone all night. But for how many nights? Without sustenance hope turns and begins to feed on itself. New phrases come to mind: "Be realistic"; "Quit looking for miracles"; "Admit you are wrong and go home." When Jesus introduced the cross into the conversation with his disciples, they could not handle it—any more than we could, or can. They were not nimble on their feet, able to convert the ways of Jesus into a gospel of success, health, and happiness. That was to come later. They did not need advice on being cheerful or help toward positive thinking. They needed a glimpse through the curtain to see if this is all there is. And so he took them up a high mountain, and he was transfigured before them.

It is no less instructive to notice that Mark places the transfiguration before the cross. Some commentators have called this a misplaced resurrection story or a story of parousia at the end of time. Perhaps, but for Mark there is the manifestation of his glory, and *then* the cross. The concern here is not with chronology but with the meaning of his coming into the world and the meaning of discipleship. Mark ends with the cross. There is an empty tomb and the silence of frightened women, but there is no resurrection appearance. This does not at all mean that Mark did not believe in the resurrection of Christ. But think what it does mean. The transfigured Christ, the One to fulfill those anticipations represented by the figures of Moses and Elijah, the Son confirmed as such by heaven's voice, goes to the cross. The order is important: glory and then the cross. Were it simply cross and then glory one could lament the cross, be angered by the cross, but finally say, "in spite of" the cross, "even though" the cross, "above and beyond" the cross. Eventually Good Friday could fall away and leave only Easter.

But not for Mark. The cross is the end toward which the transfigured one moves. Easter is God's vindication of the One crucified so that it is more true that Easter serves Good Friday than that Good Friday serves Easter. It is interesting that Luke says Moses and Elijah were talking with Jesus *about his death* (Luke 9:31). Since the story moves from transfiguration to cross, the moment of greater glory, the central moment of Jesus' ministry, was at Golgotha. It was Mark's judgment upon the disciples that they had to have a special vision of a transfigured Christ to see what a Roman soldier was able to see at the crucifixion. The centurion's confession is the one clear expression of faith in Jesus Christ in this Gospel. He saw the glory in, not before or after, the crucified Jesus.

Each preacher must decide if he or she and the church are still identified with the twelve, high on visions and miracles but low on suffering and crosses. Mark's church needed to hear the message of the cross. Whether that need arose because persecutors were on the way to their assembly or because the membership had adopted a cross-less religion of glory and "heaven now" is not clear to us. What is more important, however, is the discernment as to whether the church today is to meet Christ on the mount of transfiguration or the mount of crucifixion. In a world of unspeakable misery, dislocation of lives, hunger, and oppression, there is no question as to where Christ is. He shares in that suffering. The horrible truth is that much of the church has gathered in cross-less affluence on the other mountain.

Peter said, "Let us make three booths." And the answer was "No." And the answer is still "No." Glimpses of the eschaton, the final glory, are permitted; possessing that future is not. In the exercise of our faith, the "age to come" has appropriate functions: its victory buoys hope, its judgment warns, its glory elicits praise. The church in its inspired wisdom preserved the Book of Revelation and other apocalyptic materials, not to answer questions of curiosity, such as "When shall these things be?" but to answer with a loud "Yes" the question, "Will there be a future?" But just as the past is no dwelling place for the saints, neither is the future. As dwelling places, both past and future provide escapes, immobilize the mission, and seduce the church into a kind of blessedly religious irresponsibility.

Very likely Mark's church was plagued with such futurism, such dwelling upon the eschaton not as a future but as a present possession. This may be the point of Mark's instruction in his discussion of the last days: "The end is not yet" (13:7). In our own time, there has been a noticeable increase in this theology of glory. It usually takes one of two forms. One is an over-realized eschatology, a view that empties all the future into the present. Resurrection, judgment, glory, are all here for us and in us now, without remainder in the future. The world is full of woe, but that is not our problem because we are living in glory. The other form empties the present into the future. Present mission and responsible living are evacuated in a super-preoccupation with the future. For these, the Bible contains two books: Daniel and Revelation, and these are treated like almanacs.

Peter said, "Master, it is well that we are here; let us make three booths" and possess the future now, dwell in this glory and forget yesterday's grim conversation about the cross. And suddenly the vision was gone.

Preachers, having thus cautioned and been cautioned about stealing tomorrow, about permitting a taste of the future to become an addiction, can now more comfortably turn to Paul. He, like Mark, faced extremists in the churches, but Paul refused to allow their exaggerated claims of owning the glory to push him completely off the mountain. There *is* even now, he says, a sense of glory; we are, even now, the people of the new age: "And we all, with unveiled face, beholding the glory of the Lord, are being changed into his likeness from one degree of glory to another; for this comes from the Lord who is the Spirit" (2 Cor. 3:18).